Manhattan Beach
CHRONICLES

Manhattan Beach
CHRONICLES

Jan Dennis

THE History PRESS

Published by The History Press
Charleston, SC 29403
www.historypress.net

All images in this volume are from the author's collection.

First published 2012

Manufactured in the United States

ISBN 978.1.60949.908.2

Library of Congress CIP data applied for.

Notice: The information in this book is true and complete to the best of our knowledge. It is offered without guarantee on the part of the author or The History Press. The author and The History Press disclaim all liability in connection with the use of this book.

Contents

Acknowledgements

An appreciative thank you goes to Heidi Maerker, CEO/President of the El Segundo Herald Publications. These articles were originally published from 2009 into 2011 in the *Manhattan Beach Sun* newspaper, part of Herald Publications newspaper group, located in El Segundo, California. The *Manhattan Beach Sun* can be found online at www.heraldpublications.com.

Putting together historical columns for a community that just celebrated its 100th year of incorporation takes many hours of compiling, organizing and researching many sources. My appreciation and acknowledgments go to those many citizens who supplied photographs from private collections, as well as brochures, maps and papers.

The text in the columns and photographs has been arranged in chronological order to give the reader the feeling of the city's creation and progression. Much of the information in this book was first revealed or recounted in different order in my six prior books.

These acknowledgments would not be complete without expressing my gratitude to Jerry Roberts, commissioning editor of The History Press, for his help with the development of this volume.

Introduction

Throughout this volume we will introduce several of the elements that make Manhattan Beach, California, one of the much desired and tranquil residential addresses in the Los Angeles area.

Sixteen miles from what is now Manhattan Beach lies the city of Los Angeles, founded in 1781. However, not until the Santa Fe Railroad laid tracks passing through this area in 1888 would there be real interest in developing the virtues of these four square miles. Potential settlers were drawn to the South Bay area through brochures published by development firms such as the Redondo Beach and Centinela-Inglewood Land Companies.

Originally, the land on which today's city is located was a broad series of sand dunes on an elevated shoreline that stretched from Playa del Rey to Redondo Beach. Over the years, the topography of the sand dunes has changed.

Transportation routes in the late 1800s were sparse, especially in the undeveloped area of Manhattan Beach. In 1897, the Potencia Townsite Company purchased the Manhattan Beach waterfront, which was slowly becoming the downtown site. A few years later, in 1901, John Shirley Ward, president of the company, arranged for a siding on the Santa Fe rail line, providing a landing for supplies, machinery and equipment brought in for the construction of the first pier.

This was followed by the Pacific Electric Railway, known as the "Red Car," in 1903.With better transportation, people could live near the shore yet work in Los Angeles or other areas in the L.A. Basin. It would not

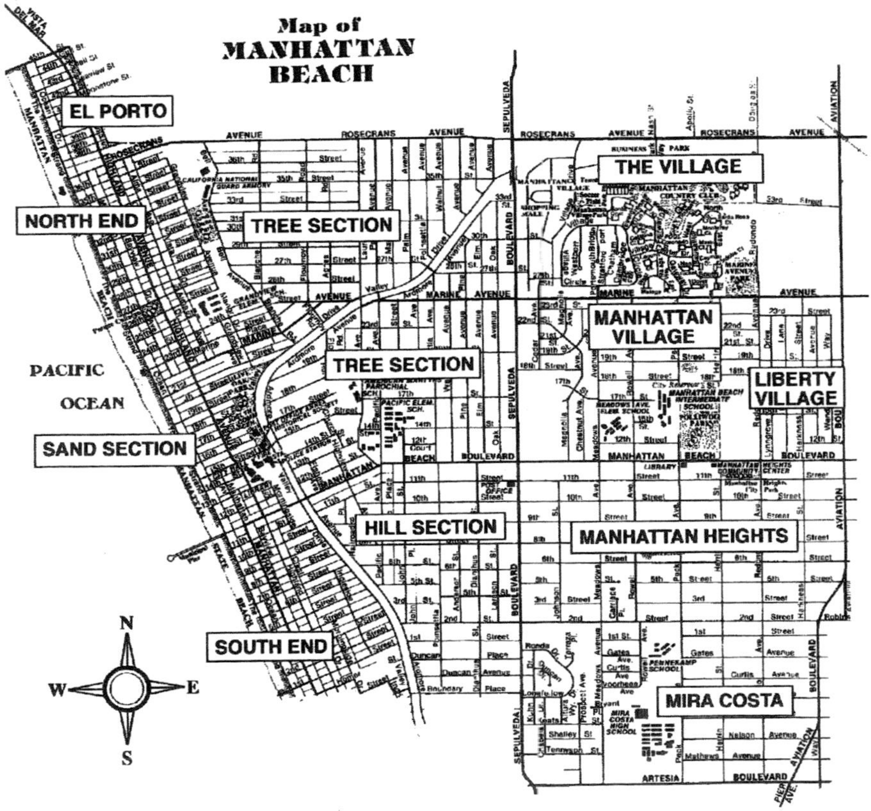

The neighborhoods of Manhattan Beach are seen here. Note the Manhattan Beach Pier at the end of Manhattan Beach Boulevard.

be until after World War II, with returning GIs and an increase in the aircraft and space industries, that dramatic increases occurred in the community's population and development and housing patterns that are reflected today.

The clear skies, dry air, little or no humidity and comfortable nights characterize much of the weather through the years. Stormy westerly winds are out of the north, and a subtropical high-pressure belt is located to the south. The temperature in Manhattan Beach does not vary as much as in the surrounding areas due to the temperate effect of the ocean and the sea breeze, keeping the winters warmer and summers cooler. It is the combination of these factors and the people who choose to live here that makes the community a "little bit of heaven on earth."

Today, as in the past, through social activities, education and business, as well as participation in local and community government, the city and its citizens strive to create a family-oriented town with stability and pride for future generations.

Chapter 1
Early Years

First Peace Officer

In 1881, several years prior to the incorporation of what is now Manhattan Beach, the nation was reading of the shootout at the O.K. Corral in Tombstone, Arizona. In 1901, when the first survey map of the Manhattan Beach town site was filled, Butch Cassidy and his gang were holding up steam trains and robbing banks, with law enforcement in hot pursuit.

There were various titles for the guardians of the peace: town marshal, county sheriff, state or territorial ranger and federal marshal. A quote by the famous sheriff Bat Masterson described these men very simply as "just ordinary men who could shoot straight and had the most utter courage and perfect nerve and for the most part, a keen sense of right and wrong."

In the late 1800s, unlike many of the other towns in Southern California that were very settled and thriving, there was little need for law enforcement in the yet undeveloped area that would eventually become the city of Manhattan Beach. The terrain along the ocean coastline was but shifting sand dunes with the landscape covered with scrub brush and flowers, and wildlife as the only inhabitants. In the early 1900s, the population began to grow with the subdivisions of the town sites. This led to a rising movement for the territory to petition to become its own town out from under the control of the City of Los Angeles.

On December 2, 1912, with returns counted by the County Board of Supervisors, it was agreed that the territory was a duly incorporated municipal corporation of the sixth class, under the name and style of "City of Manhattan Beach," becoming a self-governing community with an elected board of trustees. On December 7, 1812, Secretary of State Frank C. Jordan endorsed the findings.

The newly incorporated town, with a population of approximately six hundred, many of whom were only summer residents, was quick to put in place its own lawman. To our knowledge, there were no shootouts in early Manhattan Beach, but at the second meeting of the board of trustees, the first peace officer was appointed. Fred W. Petway became the city marshal, as well as the first fire fighting enforcement officer. Petway was on call twenty-four hours a day, seven days a week, with little equipment or training for the apprehension of lawbreakers. The city paid so poorly for the position that Marshal Petway was obliged to work odd jobs to supplement his wage.

As for law and order in the new town, Frank C. Hill was selected as city attorney. The first law enforcement case occurred in February 1913, with a disturbance of the peace charged against Joseph E. Hastings. Citizen Hastings had been arrested by Marshal Petway, found guilty and fined $15.99 by Judge C.E. Jenkins.

Little is known about the early criminal element in the community. Nevertheless, there is one story that has been documented by many early settlers. It tells of the Marshal being notified of an intruder at the Daugherty home. The Marshal called for help to arrest the prowler. After the capture, and since the town was absent a jail, the prisoner was transported in a wagon to nearby Hermosa Beach. During the trip, the assailant jumped out and began running. Marshal Petway ordered him to halt, then, as the man continued running, Petway fired his shotgun and hit the prisoner in the leg. Instead of jail, the fleer was taken to a Redondo Beach hospital. After learning he did not have the authority to use the weapon, Marshal Fred W. Petway, upset, promptly resigned his position.

GENERAL WILLIAM STARKE ROSECRANS

As Sepulveda Boulevard continued to develop into a tax stream for the city's coffers, Rosecrans Avenue on the west side of Sepulveda developed into residential housing. It would take many years before the east side of Rosecrans became a retail/office service area.

Rosecrans Avenue is the oldest street in Manhattan Beach that has retained its original identification. As it is with the naming of many streets, our northern boundary was named after a prominent personality.

William Starke Rosecrans was born on September 10, 1819, in Kingston, Ohio. Graduating from West Point in 1842 as a second lieutenant, a year later he was appointed as an assistant professor of philosophy and engineering at West Point. After an assignment in New England, Rosecrans resigned his commission in 1854 and went into private life, practicing engineering and architecture in Cincinnati and later in western Virginia.

Those who may be students of American Civil War history will know that Rosecrans served as an Ohio volunteer under G.B. McClellan. Brigadier General Rosecrans won many battles and replaced McClellan as commander in the Department of Ohio. He later became major general of volunteers and succeeded D.C. Buell in command of the Army of the Cumberland, only to be relieved of his command in 1863 after he was defeated by General Braxton Bragg's Confederate forces in the battle of Chickamauga. He was later assigned to command the Department of Missouri. Rosecrans resigned from the United States Army on March 28, 1867.

After an outstanding service record, Brigadier General Rosecrans served as United States Minister to Mexico and headed mining operations in Mexico and California in the 1870s. He served two terms in Congress as a representative from California and later served as register of the United States Treasury from 1885 to 1893.

Upon retiring to California, the family settled in Lawndale. Rosecrans himself moved to Redondo Beach, where he lived at the 225-room Hotel Redondo—a luxury installation that had been built in 1890. It was beautifully maintained with many features and activities for its guests, as well as a spectacular view overlooking the Redondo harbor. Mr. William S. Rosecrans remained there until he died on March 11, 1898.

Extending several miles east of Manhattan Beach, the Rosecrans Corridor has been an inland transportation route from the early days of the San Gabriel Mission Indians. Like Sepulveda Boulevard, the dirt road was lined on either side with eucalyptus trees, planted as windbreaks by the Los Angeles Board of Supervisors.

Improvements began on Rosecrans Avenue with the development in 1911 of the Standard Oil Refinery, located in El Segundo at Manhattan Beach's north boundary. Standard Park on the south side of Rosecrans in Manhattan Beach had been laid out shortly after the beginning of the refinery's development. The Interstate Realty and Improvement Co. was

In 1926, it was not unusual for the children of the house to care for farm animals. Little Charlene Modisett feeds the family's chickens in the backyard of their home, located at 1036 Rosecrans Avenue, now the location of the Chevron station.

selling building lots, 40 by 135 feet, in the park for only one dollar per week, with no interest, no taxes, no extras, reasonable building restrictions and free certificate of title.

The park took in the area of what is now the Tree Section: south of Rosecrans Avenue, north of Manhattan Beach Boulevard, east to Sepulveda Boulevard and west to approximately Blanch Road. The price of a lot ranged from $275 to $350, with only $5 down and all payments, except the first, made to the City and County Bank of Los Angeles. To our knowledge, the first structure to be built on Rosecrans here in town was in 1911, located at 574.

One of the area's residents, Captain H.C. Coe, owned property near the Standard Oil Company's holdings. There he owned a grocery store on Rosecrans. He had been a river man in charge of some of the largest boats plying the Columbia River and was one of the founders of the Hood River Territory. The good captain was elected president of the city's board of trustees in 1914, where he worked to improve the Standard Park area, which was struggling to get the amenities of gas and water lines. Roads in the area were still mostly sand.

In April 1914, Ordinance 79 was passed by the board of trustees for the widening of Rosecrans. Standard Oil in El Segundo to the north also

This 1929 view looks eastward at the intersection of Rosecrans and Highland Avenue. At this time, Rosecrans defined the northern boundary of the town. The Metlox sign, eighteen feet long with sixteen-inch letters in light, cream color, hung directly over the center of Highland Avenue.

pledged a thirty-foot strip of land in order to complete the project. However, it would not be paved. In 1915, with Ordinance 155, Thirty-seventh Street was renamed to Rosecrans Avenue from The Strand to Highland Avenue. Prior to this time, the road was but a wooden-planked walk to Bell Road. Beginning in 1921, several other ordinances were put into place to guard and curb various portions of Rosecrans.

Santa Fe Railroad and Developers

By the end of the 1880s, the Atchison, Topeka and Santa Fe Railroad Company played an important part in the development of the area. However, the main purpose of the railroad was to carry freight to the Redondo Beach harbor. The tracks passed through Manhattan Beach on a strip of land now known as Veterans Park, located between Valley Drive and Ardmore Avenue.

North of Center Street (now Manhattan Beach Boulevard) stood a small freight platform with two seats back-to-back covered by a roof. This structure served as a rail station. There were trains running to and from Redondo Beach by way of Inglewood. The return trips left Redondo at 10:17 a.m.

and at 7:15 p.m. When debarking from the train at Manhattan Beach, people had to plow through the sand, as there were no streets.

Potential settlers were drawn to the South Bay by brochures published by the development firms, such as the Redondo Beach and Centinela-Inglewood Land Companies. The pamphlets expounded on the virtues of this newfound area. A booklet entitled "The Pacific Homeland," published in 1888, described the adventure of the train trip: "Across a little valley with wild flowers of brilliant and varied hues. Oh, what a lovely series of views are here presented as we are whirled southward along the hillside and parallel to the shore; and finally as we make a turn allowing us to look ahead from the car window we exclaim at the beautiful alignment of the shore and the picturesque effect of the headland and Point Vincente beyond."

Early resident Ethel Horner Launer described a day in 1900: "We walked on down the beach, passing the high sand dunes located in the vicinity of Highland Avenue. There was just a wide expanse of sand, dotted with little bushes of lupines, sand verbenas and tallow primroses. I do not remember any buildings at all. We only saw two or three people and they were walking along the beach. We really explored the area that day."

Prior to the development of the downtown area, potential settlers arrived from Hermosa Beach by way of horse and buggy driven over the hard-packed sand. John A. Merrill's office building appears in the upper left, and the original wooden pier is in the lower left.

Many personalities appeared in the early years of the town. While some were summer visitors, most were investors selling and reselling the land west of the railroad tracks, now the location of downtown. Land speculators included Parvin Wright and his wife, Cora; the Potencia Townsite Company in 1897, with John Shirley Ward as president and H.S.G. McCarthy as secretary, both from Pasadena; and later, in 1901, John A. Merrill with four other men, two being his brothers, forming the Manhattan Beach Company. Several developers arranged for special railroad cars to bring prospective land buyers into the area. One such man was George H. Peck Jr., who took great pride in his native California heritage and the accomplishments of his family.

George Peck Jr. and Early Land Sales

The early developers of Manhattan Beach announced their intents to operate and maintain waterworks, as well as electric lighting, heating and power plants. The Merrills and their associates in the Manhattan Beach Company made the first mention of the intent to install, own and operate telephone lines.

On March 19, 1902, Fremont Hokerman, civil engineer, filed the first survey map for John Merrill, president of the Manhattan Beach Townsite. The property was located from Neptune Avenue, now First Street, to Thirteenth Street, east to the railroad tracks, now Ardmore Avenue, and west to The Speedway, now Ocean Drive.

The southern portion of what is now known as Manhattan Beach developed faster than the north section. The reason is unclear, but with the formation of the F.S. Daughterty, Highland Beach Company and George H. Peck Company, land sales escalated in the north as well.

George Huntington Peck Jr. (1857–1940) was one of the best-known figures in the city's history. George Jr. was born in San Francisco and spent his youth in Los Angeles. He became a brakeman for the railroad, where he met his first wife, Oliva Matilda Mitchell, a telegraph operator. After moving to San Pedro, Peck was extremely busy with many land developments, and the family name became legendary. Many of San Pedro's parks and streets are named after family members. The Peck summer home in Manhattan Beach, located at 2620 Alma Avenue (the street named after his daughter), was built to show what future land buyers could build in the area. The home still stands and is now occupied by Peck's granddaughter, Mrs. Betty Mallery.

George Huntington Peck Jr., a developer in San Pedro, Manhattan Beach and elsewhere, maintained his summer residence in Manhattan Beach.

One of the earliest accounts of entering this wonderland was that of Fred W. Horner and his family. In 1902, Mr. Horner and a group of people were interested in seeing the newly promoted Merrill development and came by way of the Santa Fe Railroad. This group's visit proved successful for the Manhattan Beach Company, which had subdivided a tract of land from First Street to Center Street, and from The Strand to Highland Avenue. Mr. Horner bought Lot 3, Block 71, for $180, and his first tax bill from the county was .90 cents. After the house was finished, the following year's taxes were $1.35.

The developer erected four other homes that summer of 1902: northeast of The Strand and Eighth Street, which was later purchased by Mr. and Mrs. Charlie Barker, owners of Barker Brothers Furniture Company; southwest corner of The Strand and Eleventh Street, owned by Mrs. Winston; the second lot west of Manhattan Avenue between Eleventh and Tenth Streets, which is now part of Becker's Bakery; and on Manhattan Avenue between Eleventh and Tenth Streets.

At this time, two commercial structures were erected on Manhattan Avenue: a small restaurant located at 109 Center Street (now Manhattan Beach Boulevard), which was later the meeting place of the first board of trustees, and a large, two-story, brick structure on the corner of Center Street and Manhattan Avenue owned by James H. Young. The building served as a general store, meeting place and post office, and it contained the only telephone in town. The second floor held the hotel, with rooms for rent.

Living in Manhattan in those days was an adventure.

The "Red Car" Arrives

With the advent of the Los Angeles Pacific Company railroad system came sightseers, developers and real estate people to the shore.

The trolley, better known as the "Red Car," was the brainchild of two enterprising young men from Arizona: Moses Hazeltine Sherman and Eli P. Clark. Seeing the possibilities of the growing West, the two gentlemen wasted no time and soon became household names in Southern California.

In 1902, work on a double-track, narrow-gauge, electric rail line began down the coast via Playa del Rey to Redondo Beach harbor. The line was laid where the bike path is now located.

There were five stops, all parallel along the sand in Manhattan Beach. The most heavily used stations were at Twenty-second Street, now Marine Avenue, and Center Street, now Manhattan Beach Boulevard. The other stops were at Peck's Pier, Peck's Beach and Verano Beach, now Fourteenth Street.

The new transportation brought an atmosphere of excitement to the area. One-time resident Mrs. Edna A. Bach relayed this feeling:

> *In those days, it was quite a thrill to ride the big red Pacific Electric streetcar. Arriving in Manhattan every hour, each car was greeted by a very jovial*

This Pacific Electric Railway "Red Car" is shown on its way through Manhattan Beach toward Hermosa Beach and then Redondo Beach. During the 1930s, Red Cars attained speeds up to sixty-five miles per hour.

personality in the person of Mr. William Schmidt (Smith), who was a real estate broker with an office on the corner of Center Street and The Strand.

Everyone was welcomed by a hearty handshake and a tail-wagging dachshund, who proudly wore a collar especially engraved with her name—Katrina Louisa Bismark Schmidt. A donkey and cart also awaited arrival of the red cars. Owned by Jean Price, it would cart your suitcases over the hills of sand for 25 cents.

The sand created special problems for the rail passengers. Sand covered the rails, so crews of Mexican laborers were kept constantly busy cleaning the tracks, causing arrival schedules to be delayed for hours at a time. People often fell when encountering the sandy boardwalks when stepping from the train.

The boardwalks were not only kept free from sand, but the boards were also maintained. When out for a stroll, residents would carry a small pail of nails and a hammer to tack down any loose boards that they might encounter. This was one way to protect each other from danger.

The "Red Car" system would stay intact for some thirty-seven years. It was very important to Manhattan Beach residents because it meant they could work in Los Angeles and retain year-round homes at the beach. However, if one lived within a few blocks of the tracks, the rumbling noises and the dimming of electric power every time a train went by were definite disadvantages.

EARLY GROWTH SLOW

Growth in Manhattan Beach was slow compared to surrounding towns, but it was steady. One example of progress was the founding of the Community Church.

In 1902, a group of residents felt the need for religious services, not only for adults but for their children as well. Charles H. Barker, one of the three Barker brothers who owned Barker Brothers Furniture in downtown Los Angeles, volunteered the family summer home, located at the corner of Eighth Street and The Strand, for a meeting to form a Sunday school. By 1906, a small, wood-framed church stood at Ninth Street and Highland Avenue. The church served as a sanctuary for its congregation and housed the town's school.

By 1912, with six hundred inhabitants residing within the boundaries of the proposed municipal corporation, it was determined to set an election to free the area from the jurisdiction of the City of Los Angeles.

Mr. and Mrs. Charles H. Barker's summer home was located at 800 The Strand. It was one of the homes built by John A. Merrill, owner of the Manhattan Beach Company.

An act to provide for the organization, incorporation and government of municipal corporations was approved by the California Legislature on March 13, 1883, giving voters the right to petition to become a city. After the necessary signatures were obtained, Captain C.E. Jenkins and eighty-five other qualified residents presented a petition to the Los Angeles County Board of Supervisors on September 30, 1912. Those opposed to incorporation also had their petitions read into the record, and a further hearing was set for 10:00 a.m. on October 12, 1912.

The supervisors established the boundaries of the proposed municipal corporation and set the election date for November 25, 1912, to determine whether the town should be incorporated.

In the election, a total of 127 votes were cast. Returns were counted on December 2, 1912, with 95 in favor of incorporation and 32 against. Voters also selected the new town's officers. Mr. Henry E. Campbell received 95 votes and Mr. William Smith 92 for four-year terms on the board of trustees. Others were elected to two-year terms.

At the same meeting of the supervisors, on a motion by Supervisor Nellis, seconded with a unanimous "aye," it was ordered that all of the territory situated in the County of Los Angeles, State of California and within the boundaries so described was a duly incorporated municipal corporation of the sixth class, under the name and style of "City of Manhattan Beach."

On December 6, 1912, H.J. Lelande, county clerk and ex officio clerk of the Board of Supervisors, certified that the copy of the original minutes of the Board of Supervisors, from December 2, 1912, were full, true and correct.

The endorsed findings were filed in the office of Secretary of State Frank C. Jordan on December 7, 1912. With the affidavit completed, the township was officially recognized as an incorporated city. So began a new independent town on the shore of Santa Monica Bay.

Life on the Dunes

It could be a five-hour trip from Los Angeles to Manhattan Beach when bringing a load of furniture to a new home. Living at the beach was a refuge from the city heat. However, women found other stressful encounters waiting for them in the beach wilderness.

Summer cottages were being built on the sand dunes, but few owners spent the winter months. In the winter of 1904, there were twelve permanent families living in town. That same year, Mrs. Lucy A. Horner, who had come to Los Angeles in 1888 from Ohio, brought her two children, Ethel and James, to a small, two-bedroom summer cottage to become permanent residents. The young family found the first winter at the beach extremely lonely. Women had little opportunity to meet, for they were isolated geographically and social life was nonexistent.

Residents had to contend not only with blowing sand but also the wildlife of the area. In 1907, the George Fischer family purchased eight acres and built a four-room summer cottage at 1501 Pacific Avenue. At the time, going out to collect cut wood for a cottage stove could be an adventure in itself. Needing wood, Mrs. Fischer discovered a family of what she thought were badgers. She returned to the house, rolled up some small raw hamburger balls, salted them and presented them to the badgers only to find that they were not badgers but skunks.

When it came to washing the family's clothes, most housewives washed by hand, utilizing a tin tub and carrying hot water from the kitchen stove. The articles of clothing were then hung on a line to dry. However, Mrs. Vogel, who lived at the corner of Seventeenth Street and Pacific Avenue, was the proud owner of a large flywheel washing machine. When the morning breeze picked up, the flywheel would be set in place to activate the machine. The sun was called on to dry the garments, and ironing was done with the use of a flat iron that had been heated on the stove.

Water was another problem for the early settlers, who dealt with not only high sulfur content but also limited water pressure. A tank and well were

The Municipal Water Plant with a 145-foot-high tower having a capacity of sixty thousand gallons of water. The pumping house and tank stood between Sixth and Eighth Streets at Sepulveda Boulevard. The system was utilized until 1942, when the city joined the Metropolitan Water District and acquired water from the Colorado and Feathered River projects.

located on the sand dune at Highland Avenue and Sixteenth Street, and another well was on the hill around Thirteenth Street and Highview Avenue. There was also a water tank on the Miller tract at Thirty-first Street and Pacific Avenue, where residents could obtain water and carry it back to their homes in buckets.

After the paving of Highland, the Sixteenth Street well was abandoned, and water was supplied by the Hermosa Beach Land and Water Company at a cost of ten dollars a year per user. When the pressure went down, homeowners inspected the rushed pipe that lay in the sand and repaired any leaks that were found. Citizens complained about a lack of water. They felt they had suffered at the hands of the company and wanted a new system.

Many residents made their dissatisfaction known, but one of the most dramatic was Mrs. Annie Threlkeld. It was said she wept enough tears to fill a bucket on the loss of her finest chickens. She claimed they perished because of the lack of water. Mrs. Threlkeld owned most of the frontage of what is now John Street. In following years, the small beach community had its own water system, with the Municipal Water Plant located on what is now Sepulveda Boulevard between Sixth and Eighth Street.

Mrs. Clara Auchmoody, whose husband served on the board of trustees, ran a thirteen-acre farm in the "back country" known as Goat Hill—so named for the herd of goats she owned. In later years, she built a two-story home at 100 Sepulveda Boulevard as well as a gift shop at 110 Sepulveda, just north of her home. She also grew potatoes, claiming she sold sixteen thousand pounds each season. Dubbed a "farmerette" at the California State Fruit Association conference in 1914, she was a hit at the event and gave credit for being a first-class "Murphy" (potato) grower. Life on the farm was a happy adventure until the water rates increased at the end of 1914.

A Day at the Beach

At the turn of the twentieth century, the preparations for a day at the beach were relatively simple. You determined your method of transportation and then stocked a picnic basket with ample food. Arriving at the beach, you perhaps buried a watermelon in the sand at the water's edge, and in two or three hours, you would enjoy its chilled juiciness.

The logistics for a summer at the beach were considerably more difficult, and for year-round residents, keeping house on the sand dunes was a real

In the summer of 1914 on the beach, Lucey Caley displayed the condition of her living quarters. Ordinance #320 on May 17, 1928, outlawed any person to erect, maintain or occupy a tent on any part of the beach that was west of The Strand. If the law were not obeyed, the penalty was a $300 fine or three months in jail.

challenge. With deep sand, no streets and no utilities, the population was sparse. In the winter months, the sand could drift to the window ledges, like snow. By 1905, board sidewalks had been installed in what is now the downtown area, making foot travel much easier.

There were a few houses, but people did live in tents both on the beach and east of the railroad tracks. Basic supplies could be obtained from the corner store at Manhattan Avenue and Center Street (which became Manhattan Beach Boulevard) and at the Grant Store, located at the corner of what is now Aviation Way and Artesia Boulevard. It was a far jaunt on foot or pony, but one could journey to Redondo Beach to shop for such items as kerosene for lamps or gasoline for cooking stoves. Ralphs Grocery in Los Angeles would pack orders in large wooden boxes and place them on the Santa Fe train, to be unloaded on the Manhattan Beach platform just north of Center Street.

From the small farms east of Sepulveda Boulevard, residents could purchase eggs, butter, chickens, rabbits and sometimes fresh meat. From a horse-drawn, light spring wagon, an old German man delivered fresh vegetables, fruit and honey. He drove through town twice a week in summer and once a week in winter, selling produce from his farm in the "back country."

People could also go up to the Cotrell family farm, located at the corner of Pacific Avenue and Center Street, to purchase freshly grown watermelon, cantaloupe, tomatoes, corn and peanuts. For one dollar per acre per year, the Cotrells rented the land on which they lived and grew crops.

Food was plentiful if one liked fresh fish and clams. All kinds of fish and shellfish were pulled from the sea: yellowtail, bass, smelt and barracuda. Soft-shell crabs were caught for bait by the young people, who sold their catch for three to five cents a dozen to the man who ran the bait stand on the pier.

Fishing was done from the old wooden pier, beginning at sunrise and lasting to late afternoon, by both adults and children. Many times the haul of the day would be taken home, where the women would prepare the evening meal.

One of the hardest tasks was disposing of garbage and trash. Children of the families often had the chore of digging a hole in the sand to bury trash. The size of the hole would depend on the length of stay at the location. Upon returning the next weekend or summer, another hole was dug and the process repeated. Due to the strong winds, especially in winter months, trash would frequently be found uncovered and scattered across the dunes.

THE NEPTUNIAN CLUB

In 1909, nine ladies in the community rallied together in good spirits with Mrs. Jessie Smith, who saw a need for an organization to serve the new town and make life more meaningful. Jessie was elected the first president of the newly formed club. It was noted that when the club members met, the ladies often appeared on the boardwalks dressed to the nines and carrying parasols.

Over the years, the Neptunian Women's Club has lobbied hard and played a great role in the development of this town. By 1916, with a membership of approximately twenty, the group joined the California Federation of Women's Clubs.

It was unfortunate that Mrs. B. Jessie Smith, who passed away in April 1913, did not live to see the wonderful work that the club would accomplish. She died from complications of diabetes, namely gangrene. Insulin was not developed until the 1920s, so she did not have the benefit of that treatment. It was reported that her death certificate was the first to be issued in the city of Manhattan Beach.

In 1916, a luncheon was held honoring Mrs. Birdie Emery, who taught first and second grade at Center Street School. Other ladies were all members of the Neptunian Women's Club. This photo was taken in front of Mrs. Withers's home at 604 Nineteenth Street. *Back row:* Mrs. R. Castile. *Second row:* Mrs. R. Gardner, Mrs. Klarquist, Mrs. F.M. Sinsabaugh, Mrs. Birdie Emery. *Front row:* Katherine Withers, Helen Sinabaugh, Alyce Castile and Jerry Withers, who in 1956 became police chief in Manhattan Beach.

As the club grew in attendance, other ladies took on civic and social leadership. Mrs. Maude Withers was a legend in her own right, often referred to as "the mother of Manhattan Beach."

Maude Amy Conwell hailed from Havana, Illinois, and, with her family, moved to the Los Angeles area when she was twelve. After schooling, she entered the business world as a secretary at Barker Brothers store and, in 1905, married J.H. Withers. In 1909, the couple moved to Manhattan Beach and became well known for their enduring work in the community.

In February 1909, an article appeared in the *New York World* newspaper detailing the eyewitness account by William and Reuben Withers of the assassination of President Lincoln. Their interviews were published around the world. The Witherses served in the Civil War, were members of the Sixty-second Pennsylvania Volunteers and were also members of the Ford's Theater orchestra. Their father, Colonel William Withers, was the director who blocked John Wilkes Booth's flight from the theater and was stabbed by the assassin.

After the death of Mr. J.H. Withers, nephew of Colonel Withers and Maude's husband, Maude shared the many newspaper articles of the witness with local periodicals, which again published the details of the event. Maude's work in the community included being a member of the Manhattan Beach Community Church, president of the Neptunian Club, production chairman of the Red Cross and chair of the South Bay Republican Women's Club. She even spent time with the Lions Club before women were admitted. Her involvement spanned sixty years of civic and social leadership and service.

While concerned with civic promotion projects, the women of the community were also concerned with the well being of the children in town and their education. They called the public's attention to the absence of a school district in Manhattan Beach and volunteered to contact the county superintendent of schools to learn the requirements in order to establish one. On February 3, 1913, the Manhattan Beach School District was formed after the Los Angeles County Board of Supervisors accepted the resident petition. Prior to this date, all area schools were a part of the eleven-thousand-acre Wiseburn School District, which had been formed in 1896. The new district serviced only the lower grades, as high school students attended Redondo Beach High School.

The educational philosophy of the community was to help each child function at the maximum of his or her competence. With local control, the voters of Manhattan Beach elected three citizens to establish and form the school district. It was determined to have the finest elementary educational system in the nation. On September 8, 1913, fifteen pupils attended class at the Community Church as part of the new system.

ARRIVAL OF SCHOOLS

In 1913, residents in Manhattan Beach were striving to develop a winning school district. The three trustees, J.C. Reinhard, Walter Nelson and L.J. Price held their first business meeting in April 1913 and decided to hold an election to vote a bond issue of $23,000 in order to purchase land and erect a school building. A total of twenty-one votes were cast, all were in favor of the bond, constituting the necessary two-thirds majority vote for its passage.

By November, $6,500 was paid for several acres of land, now the location of the Pacific Elementary School at the corner of Pacific Avenue and Manhattan Beach Boulevard. The new four-classroom school was built in the shape of an *L* by Mr. W.M. Bell, who had submitted the lowest bid of $10,235 for framing and $11,335 for the tile work.

With the completion of the structure, Center School was dedicated on April 30, 1914, with an enrollment of forty-three students attending the following year. There were two professional teachers for a term of nine and a half months. At a salary of ninety dollars per month, Miss Bertie Miller was the first primary and middle grade teacher. The principal and upper grade teacher was a gentleman by the name of Mr. Cyrus Quick, at a salary of ninety-five dollars per month. Mr. Quick's daughter, Miss Lois Quick, who was not paid, conducted grammar school music classes.

As one can imagine, the early school development was not an easy task, with the trustees not seeing eye-to-eye and having as many as two to four new members per year. There were also the demands from other outside groups. It was a time in history when school board districts did not accept female members. However, due to disagreements and a lack of cooperation, the first female trustee member in Manhattan Beach was seated. Mrs. E. Clark remained a member and became the first female president of the district from 1916 through 1919.

By the end of the 1919 school year, the board had a budget of $8,505.94 with which to operate the following year. The staff consisted of three teachers at a salary of $97.00 per month. Women played an enormous role in the development and education of the students, yet very few women held administrative positions.

Teachers were held to a very high standard; they could not marry or smoke, in fact anti-smoking clauses were written into their contracts. They wore dresses because slacks were not only banned but also considered almost sinful. Wearing pants did not come into vogue until World War II. As for hairstyles, it would not be until the movie star Clara Bow bobbed her hair that hair bobbing was accepted in school circles. It was part of the teachers' agreement with the district that they live in town. Due to the lack of housing, they often would board with families in the community or lodge at local boarding houses. Their contract excluded any health benefits, and they were expected to teach Sunday school at the local community church.

The teaching profession was one of a few vocations a woman of this period in time could pursue, as it was felt that the only proper place for a woman was the home and her only proper work was caring for her husband and children. There were few women in business, for the thrust of their energy was put into social and philanthropic endeavors. However, as more and more women attained higher education, they went into the workplace and the commercial world.

FIRE DEPARTMENT

While schools, the police department and utilities were supported by the town, firefighting was last on the list of town improvements. Having a lack of water and few water hydrants, fires were fought by an all-volunteer group of men who did their best to protect the new town. Fire districts were created, and when help was needed to fight a blaze, an alarm was sounded and anyone in the district or vicinity was expected to help.

In November 1914, Ordinance No. (113) was established, "regulating construction, repairing, and removing buildings for protection from fire and explosions." Over the years, amendments have been made to the ordinance relating to the fire districts.

Fires in town were often fought by the Hermosa Beach Fire Department. The circumstances surrounding a fire in February 1921 may have changed the town's previous attitude about the need for a fire department. It all started at 1148 Manhattan Avenue, when an electrical switch was left on.

Residents trying to call the Hermosa Beach Department went to three or four houses before they found a telephone. Five local firemen made it to the scene within four minutes of hearing the alarm, in spite of a gale-force wind blowing directly against them and streets almost completely covered by the swirling sand. Even though the wind whipped the flames, the fire was extinguished in rapid time.

At the December 1921 board of trustee's meeting, the need for fire protection was decided and the water superintendent was instructed to purchase two glass nozzles and a three-hundred-foot hose. The hose was stored in the city hall. When a call for help was received by the city hall, it called the Manhattan Hardware and Plumbing Company to bring its Model T Ford pick-up truck, hook up the hose reel and attend to the fire. This only worked if the truck was not out on a delivery.

It was determined this was not an efficient way to put out a fire. In February 1923, several local citizens got together and organized the Lion Tamers Club, basically a social men's group that was very involved with the community. The members' intent was to form a volunteer fire department. One of the longest-standing members was J.H. Wilkens, who would serve as a volunteer fireman for the next forthy-three years, until his death in 1966. Hardware store owner W.W. Peppers was the first president of the Lion Tamers and fire chief, until he was replaced by Harry Hicks in 1924.

Hicks remained chief until August 1930. During Hicks's term as chief, the city purchased for $1,069.25 the first chemical Model T truck. The truck

Chief H.L. Hicks, the only paid member of the fire department, driving the new Seagrave pumper out of the old city hall, which was the location of the first fire department.

was modified with two chemical tanks, five hundred feet of 2.5-inch hose, two ladders, a hand-operated siren to call volunteers, six turnout coats and two fire helmets.

While organized fire fighting was a sign of progress, one of the most significant signs was the Manhattan Beach Development Company, a Delaware corporation formed in August 1921. It was to be involved with every aspect of community real estate development, from owning and operating hotels and cafés to building houses and commercial buildings. There were ten thousand shares of common stock. W.S. Myers, of Los Angeles, was named attorney, and C.H. Avey, also of Los Angeles, was secretary of the company.

EARLY CONTRIBUTIONS BY WOMEN

Numerous women of Manhattan Beach have worked hand in hand with the city on hundreds of civic projects improving the welfare and lifestyle of all residents. Over the past 102 years, through social work, education, business and the arts, these ladies have also added to the professional and political landscape, participating in local and county government arenas.

Today, women continue to make a strong and positive difference in the community, striving to create a safe, family-oriented town with stability and pride for the generations to come. From the beginning of the Women's Suffrage Rights Convention in 1848, women worked for the right to vote as well as participated in the development of their surroundings. By 1897, women in the South Bay were taking an active part in their communities. In Manhattan Beach, then known as Potencia, one of the first women to be involved in the community was Mrs. Cora Wright. She and her husband bought and sold land in the vicinity of what is now the Metlox shopping site and Von's Market.

With deep sand, no streets and no transportation, the population was sparse. However, there were those who battled the sand dunes in order to catch fish, dig for clams and enjoy the tranquility of the uncrowded landscape.

Prior to incorporation of this approximately four-square-mile territory, the sparsely inhabited town site was under the control of the City of Los

One of the few 1909 bungalows constructed upon the sand near the pier at Tenth Street and Manhattan Avenue. During the winter months, many of the cottages were boarded up until summer returned.

The interior of the Harold Cashin family beach cottage, then located at Sixteenth Street west of Highland Avenue.

Angeles. To appreciate the activities of the early women in this small seaside community, one has to explore the dedication of the women who saw the need for the town's incorporation and freedom from the influence of Los Angeles. Although the women in California could not vote until 1911, ten local ladies not only rocked the cradle but also rocked the boat.

Several of the ladies were the wives of men who served on the town's board of trustees, and perhaps there was much "pillow talk" about women's rights and the involvement of women in the creation of an independent Manhattan Beach. The ladies realized the need for a town-owned school system, police and fire departments and governmental self-control.

There were less hardships for women at the beach compared to life for the women of the Midwest, but compared to the lifestyle in Los Angeles or Pasadena, there were many challenges. The drifting sand could be hostile. By 1905, boardwalk sidewalks had been installed in what is now the downtown area, making foot travel in the long skirts of the day much easier than walking in the deep sand.

It would be several years before a house had indoor plumbing, gas, electricity or water. However, oil and water could be bought by the barrel at the local general store. The ladies could also purchase staples, candies, seeds for planting and sometimes fine lace. There was a system whereby the housewife would pin a dishtowel on the clothesline to indicate that she would like to have a purchase delivered from the general store. This service was brought to homes on certain days of the week.

To seek more of a variety of shops and department stores, one could travel to Redondo Beach by way of horse and buggy over the wet, hard-packed sand or ride the "Red Car." The trip would take the better part of the day. In Redondo, one could find dry goods, home supplies and perhaps a new sunbonnet.

Stock in the local store was not plentiful during the winter months, for fewer families resided here at the beach. However, supplies could be ordered from Ralphs Market in downtown Los Angeles. The order would arrive on the Santa Fe Railroad, and twenty-five cents would be paid to have the wooden boxes brought to the purchaser by horse-drawn wagon.

CLARA AUCHMOODY AND THE COST OF WATER

We introduced Mrs. Clara Auchmoody in the previous piece, a lady who was very happy on the farm and in her overalls. She felt farm life had every advantage over any other kind of life; it easily beat the city women's life. She saved her money until she could buy one acre then kept saving and trading until she eventually accumulated thirteen acres. She managed the farm alone and directed the labor of her hired man. Her husband did not like the farm life and lived in town.

In 1914, Mrs. Auchmoody had an interview with the *Los Angeles Examiner*, stating that she had the ambition to become mayor of Manhattan Beach. She had a strong concern about the water problems in town and wanted the ladies especially to observe what was going on. In November of that same year, an investigation was carried out by the City Water Commission due to numerous criticisms from property owners and taxpayers' dissatisfaction.

It was felt by Mrs. Auchmoody that the city officials, both past and present, failed to carry out the terms of the bond issue for the construction of the municipal water system. She sued based on the alleged misapplication of $6,000, which was borrowed from the water fund and only about one-third of which had been returned. In early 1916, every cent of the money was paid back to the water department.

When the water rates went up, Auchmoody refused to pay the higher rate and the city cut off water to her farm. She felt the turning off of the water was done without just cause and alleged damages in the sum of $5,000 for the loss of 796 chicks, pepper plants, cantaloupes, flowers and shrubbery.

Mr. William and Mrs. Jessie Smith at their farm, which bisected Eighth Street and Pacific Avenue. Young man not identified. Circa 1900–1910.

The complaint also alleged that she had a twenty-year contract when she purchased her land to pay 8.05 cents per one thousand gallons and that the city was obligated to furnish water at that price.

However, the city maintained it could only afford to deliver the water for ten cents for one thousand gallons, and since Mrs. Auchmoody refused to pay the higher rate, it took the action of cutting off the water supply.

It was at this time the city auditor, Mr. L.A. Hatch, sent a letter to Mrs. Auchmoody's neighbor, Mr. S.A.D. Clark, saying not to supply her with water, and that if he did, he would face a fifty-dollar fine or fifty days in jail. Auchmoody's attorney, Mr. Goldman, advised Mr. Clark to ignore the letter, for if any arrests were to take place it would result in a large damage action suit. The attorney also addressed the board of trustees, sharing that in as much Mrs. Auchmoody's husband sat on the board of trustees, more consideration should have been shown in the interruption of the farm's water supply. The court's decision declared that Mrs. Clara Auchmoody must pay the rate demanded by the city or do without water.

Mrs. Clara Auchmoody won $600 from the city in the 1920s, which she lost on the city's appeal. However, she became renowned for her lawsuits against the City of Manhattan Beach. She was also party to the first jury trial in the town, overseen by City Clerk C.E. Jenkins. The hearing was held in a building on The Strand between Manhattan Beach Boulevard and Twelfth Street. She was suing Mr. Clark because he plowed up her cantaloupe patch in a boundary dispute.

There were other women who took great interest in the development of the new town. Civic pride was projected through the activity of the Neptunian Women's Club, which was started by Mrs. Jessie Bell Smith. Mrs. Jessie B. Smith was born in England in 1857, immigrated to the United States when she was seventeen years old and, in 1885, married William Smith in Ohio prior to moving to Manhattan Beach. According to the 1900 Redondo Township U.S. census, William and Jessie Smith lived in Manhattan Beach, where Mr. Smith was listed as "farmer."

The 1910 U.S. census for Redondo Township indicated that the couple lived at the corner of Eleventh and Manhattan Avenue, and William Smith's occupation was listed as "real estate."

Jessie was active in the Eastern Star and elected as the first president of the newly formed club.

BUSINESSWOMEN

In 1913, a woman created a very successful business on the Manhattan Beach shoreline. She was the only black woman to own a business in the early days of this community's development. Mrs. Willa (known as Willie) A. Bruce had been born in Missouri, later to move to New Mexico in about 1888, where she married Mr. Charles A. Bruce. They moved to Manhattan Beach, where on February 15, 1912, the African American couple purchased, from Henry Willard, a lot located between Twenty-sixth and Twenty-seventh Streets on The Strand.

The popular Gray Gull Café Restaurant was located at 909 Manhattan Avenue and owned by Mrs. Gibson Howard, who also ran the real estate office next door. She was one of the first women to sell property in Manhattan Beach. Photo taken in 1923.

In 1915, Willie and her husband began construction of a lodge, dance hall and café for minority families. The complex was known as Bruce's Lodge, on the property now dedicated as Bruce's Beach Park. Willie did very well as a businesswoman, and in 1920, she purchased another contiguous lot to the south of the original acquisition. However, by 1926, some in the community proposed condemning the lodge property through eminent domain and converting the land into a park.

Other women who went into business in the early days of the community included Mrs. Spaulding, who ran a small country store located on the corner of Thirty-eighth Street and Highland Avenue, and Mrs. Mary Haeberlin, who was the proprietor of the notions shop in town, located on the business block on Manhattan Avenue.

There were many restaurants and cafés owned by local women. In 1923, Mrs. Maria Louise Howard opened the Gray Gull Café, a small, exclusive eatery located on Manhattan Avenue. It was well known for its extraordinary and palate-tingling meals, as Mrs. Howard prepared fresh food and fish each day. Many prominent people from Los Angeles and Pasadena who had summer homes in both Manhattan and Hermosa Beach were frequent patrons.

As increased housing demands became evident in the city, Mrs. Briggs built and opened an apartment house at Blanche Road and Rosecrans Avenue, almost at the Pacific Avenue gate of the Standard Oil Company. The building had two stories and twelve three-room, modern apartments. Businesses opened in the summer and closed in the winter. In fact, many were converted to other endeavors. One example was the Manhattan Inn, which Miss C.M. Cook and Mrs. L. Baughman used as a school that readied mentally handicapped children for mainstreaming into regular schools.

As the years went on, other notable businesswomen included Mrs. Blanche Ercole, part owner of Ercole's Café at 1101 Manhattan Avenue; Mrs. Jeanette Switzer, who met the public each day with a smile and cheery hello while working with her husband at the White Stop Café; and Mrs. E. McCameron, who opened the Manhattan Tea Gardens at 313 Eighth Street. Back in the classroom, by 1923–24, as the school population grew to 207, the faculty at the Center Street School expanded to a teaching staff of six teachers and one teacher/principal.

New female teachers received $1,300 per year, while permanent teachers received $1,750 annually for a ten-month year. Women had been teaching many years before higher education was required, but as the years went on, salaries were paid according to the type of degree or certification one received.

In 1926, Miss Aurelia Pennekamp was hired for an annual salary of $525, to serve as the first part-time nurse at the Center Street School. Known for her leadership and ability to communicate with the children, she also worked in the same capacity for many neighboring school districts. By 1946, she was employed by the Manhattan Beach School District full time, then as nurse inspector. During the mid-1950s, she was the district's health chair.

Chapter 2
1920s

Manhattan Beach Development Company

From its very beginning, the Manhattan Beach Development Company was very involved in the city. On November 4, 1921, it sponsored a "monstrous" booster celebration for the town. A week later, it announced plans to create a villa city with 420 lots. The houses were to be four- or five-room bungalows with hot and cold water, hardwood floors and stucco walls painted white. The color, city officials said, shall be "the prevailing color for the wonderful city of Manhattan Beach." This location, south of Manhattan Beach Boulevard between Crest Drive and Valley Drive, is now referred to as a "walk street" area, in which no cars are allowed to drive or park.

The following was taken from promotional material the company circulated: "From careful, conservative estimates this venture alone was expected to net 8 percent on the total capitalization of the company. Although building permits of over one-half million dollars have already been issued, Manhattan Beach is sadly in need of many commercial structures; such as stores, garages, auto accessories, gasoline stations and banking facilities. Enterprising home-seekers and progressive citizens will find many lucrative opportunities waiting."

The company owned the 3,100 feet of ocean frontage extending from First Street to Thirteenth Street, excepting 200 feet frontage at the pier. It built a $10,000 bathhouse, which had a capacity for 360 bathers to rent lockers and change clothes. It also owned a pier restaurant, which was located at the

1922, the pier and pavilion after its completion. The Manhattan Beach Development Company finished the work on the pavilion at a cost of $15,000.

head of the pier. In addition, the company was to build a $15,000 pavilion on the ocean end of the pier with a bait shop, tackle rental for fishermen and a restaurant. The outside of the building was stucco with a Spanish-tile roof and large gooseneck reflectors to light up the building so it could be seen from shore, as well as for miles out at sea.

The pier had a dubious beginning. A $75,000 bond issue had been proposed for a 1,500-foot pier at the foot of Center Street (Manhattan Beach Boulevard). However, it failed 168 to 170 in August 1914, thanks to a "Necessities Before Luxuries" campaign. The issue was revived the next year and passed in 1916. A compromise was struck for a $70,000 pleasure pier at Center Street and a $20,000 pavilion at Marine Avenue.

A.L. Harris, special engineer for the city, designed and submitted plans in 1916 stating the practical and unique reasons a round-end pier would be desirable to the California coastline. He said, "It is a feature unique to the coastline and it is much stronger against the action of the water."

The causeway was to be 1,250 feet in length, leading to a 100-foot diameter area. However, the municipal pier extended 928 feet out into the Santa Monica Bay. Because of contracting problems exacerbated by World War I, the pier was not finished until July 5, 1920. At the time, the deck spanned approximately 760 feet of water.

Following World War I, a boom in building brought many families to town. Prohibition was in effect, but it was still the age of bathtub gin and bootlegging. As women trimmed their dresses and bobbed their hair, the Victorian Age came to an end, heralding bathing suit contests and jazz.

Manhattan Beach had its share of moonshiners, inebriated drivers racing through town and flappers dancing the night away. Still, it was a family town, and it cracked down hard on anything that would disturb that image.

Auto Age

America was rushing pell-mell into the Auto Age and nowhere faster or more recklessly than in Manhattan Beach. On May 9, 1924, a car leaped thirty feet into the air, landing on the beach. Fortunately, only minor injuries resulted. Almost every week, there was some kind of traffic encounter. In August of that year, one penniless and reckless driver had to paint parking spaces for three days during what was pronounced as the "Week of the Speeders."

Another example was J. Harper, described as a person "from the large and congested city," who was speeding down Center Street (Manhattan Beach Boulevard) in his Studebaker Special when he was caught. The *Manhattan Beach News* stated, "Judge Price must have been in a terrible state of mind because he charged the fellow $500 in gold." Following sentencing, the hapless Harper was reported "to be convalescing from shock."

There were more than half a million cars in Los Angeles at the time, and people went without necessities to have a prestigious car. At the time, a driver did not have to take any tests. The only requirement for getting a license was to be able to fill out name, hair and eye color. The Automobile Association of Southern California found that incompetent drivers were the main cause of accidents.

One of the unhappiest events was the destruction of the Neptunian Memorial Rock Drinking Fountain. In 1915, Mrs. John C. Stockwell, chairman of the committee to erect a memorial fountain to Mrs. Jessie Smith, founder of the Neptunian Club, announced the club had $200 to build this memorial. The club ladies had held bake sales and sponsored weekly card parties to raise funds for the construction. Since the fountain was to be built of sea stone, each member had to bring a rock from the ocean to each club meeting. The *Manhattan Beach News* reported that everyone who went down to the beach gathered a few stones of pleasing surface and, on his or her return from the water, would toss the stones into a barrel, thus rapidly accumulating the desired rocks.

Intersection of Manhattan Beach Boulevard and Manhattan Avenue in 1920s prior to the Neptunian Memorial Fountain being destroyed.

The structure was constructed at the intersection of Manhattan Avenue and Center Street displaying cast conch shells mounted on either side by mythical fish heads topped by a trident with an electric light in the center. One side served animals, and the other side was a fountain for people. It was a tribute to the Model T era until its demise in 1928, when a tipsy Rolls Royce driver obliterated the work of love.

When the fountain was hit, the two couples in the car were on their way to the Pier End Café. They thought the light on the fountain was the pier and headed in that direction. The fountain was not repaired. However in 1990, the Neptunian Woman's Club reproduced and constructed the artifact in Polliwog Park.

Thieves found it relatively easy to steal cars. The first car stolen in Manhattan Beach was taken from a man who had parked his car in order to go swimming in the ocean. It appeared a husband and wife car thief team were chased by the marshal, who was fired upon as they fled.

Police in the 1920s

In 1924, with a population of 859, Manhattan Beach was no longer a sleepy little town, and it was time more enforcement was available to protect the residents and visitors. At this time, the board of trustees replaced the

Some of the thousands of people Chief Harry S. Boardman and his officers had to deal with during the summer season.

marshal with a police chief. Fred J. Garvin became the first Manhattan Beach Police Chief (1924–1929) and had a department consisting of one officer, Patrolman Harry S. Boardman. The chief and Boardman worked twelve-hour shifts seven days a week and were on call twenty-four hours a day.

To be a Manhattan Beach police officer meant that one had to have his own car, uniform and weapon. However, the city did buy the Henderson motorcycle that Gavin operated, paid for the red light and siren for the patrol car and furnished gas for the vehicles. There were no specific qualification requirements for employment, nor were the new police personnel given any technical instructions. Just keep the peace!

By 1925, the department was organized and fully operating, with twenty-five arrests made that year. When an officer was needed, the city clerk, who was also the sergeant, jailer and judge, would turn on a red light that hung outside of his office window. In later years, the red light was installed approximately one hundred feet above the city hall, and an air horn was installed on the side of the building. It was up to the patrolman to see the light or hear the blasting horn and then return to the department to receive his instructions. As one can imagine, this type of communication did not work should the patrolman be out of sight or earshot of city hall.

One of the biggest problems for the city and patrolmen was the adoption of the automobile for individual transportation, dramatically affecting the traffic flow and the safety of pedestrians. The beach—sun, sand, sea and sky—brought celebrities and the general public to Manhattan Beach. During the Depression decade, beach lovers could claim that, in the words of a popular song, "the best things in life are free." City officials, however, complained that most people who used the beach lived elsewhere and therefore escaped paying taxes for beach maintenance and police expenses.

Manhattan Beach at the time was promoted as the "Safest Beach in America," and with summer crowds, this caused the police department to be expanded. Chief Garvin had retired his position in 1929, and his only patrolman, Harry S. Boardman, became the new police chief. Parking problems and crowd control necessitated the hiring of more parking patrol officers. Traffic was a nightmare! Thousands of people came to the beach and onto the pier trying to catch the "Big One." Nothing could slow down this influx, not even the Great Bull Market Crash of 1929.

Bootlegging was still active and also a problem for the new chief. In the spring of 1930, officers found a three-hundred-gallon illegal still in a home at 340 Ninth Street, a block east of the Community Church. The still had been installed in a bedroom, with the tank placed in the bathroom. A gas line had been connected to the main line, bypassing the meter. Copper tubing extending approximately thirty feet south of the house led to a large galvanized tank at the side of the garage. Chief Boardman kept close surveillance of the property. However, the operators did not return, causing the still to be dismantled and taken to the station to await orders from federal authorities.

It all became too much for Chief Boardman, and he resigned in the latter part of June 1930, serving only one year as chief. Alex Haddock, who had been a member of the department for four years, became the third police chief. The department now consisted of five officers on the force, including two plainclothes officers. In order to have better contact with his patrolmen, three telephones were installed on poles around town so officers could check in with the police desk.

BUSINESSMEN ACUMEN

With the growth of the town's population and thousands of visitors each summer, more businesses were established. It was difficult indeed for a Manhattan Beach politician in the 1920s to determine what would please the fickle voters. The businessmen's ticket was swept into office in the municipal election of 1924 only to face a request from Louis Lee to have a restaurant and barber shop with three pool tables.

The board of trustees supported the new endeavor from the business angle, but the ladies of the city opposed it as being detrimental to family life. They thought pool halls were the known purveyors of alcohol and narcotics, and they feared their sons would be led astray.

Businessman U.T. Thompson defended the proposed enterprise as a legitimate business. It would, he said, have a sign out front, as required by state law, saying, "Boys under 18 years of age not admitted." As for the drugs, Thompson said, "It is true that pool halls have been closed for such acts as the above; so also have drug stores, but shall we keep drug stores our of our town on this account?" The mothers were not convinced. A special election was held after months of debate. The pool hall was defeated 211 to 178. Women's suffrage was a reality!

The pool hall may not have survived, but in 1922, Joe Ercole's small soda fountain did. At the present location, 1101 Manhattan Avenue, the soda fountain soon was turned into a full restaurant and cocktail lounge. The business and building remain today.

Business block looking north on Manhattan Avenue. A large building sat on the corner of Manhattan Avenue and Center Street, now Manhattan Beach Boulevard, circa 1920s.

Joe Ercole was a native of Asti Piedmont, Italy, and came to this country as a young man. In the early years in California, he lived in Los Angeles, where he had many different jobs. One of his talents was that of an excellent inlaid tile man. Some of his work can still be seen in the marble of the Los Angeles City Hall building.

To help promote the city's proper image, the Manhattan Beach Chamber of Commerce had been formed January 23, 1920, with the first open meeting held February 2. All were invited, with dues of six dollars for six months. The chamber's first project was to find a suitable slogan for the city. Ms. Blake Franklin of Los Angeles won with the phrase "Manhattan Beach, the Queen of the Dunes." Although Franklin did not live in Manhattan Beach, she was a property owner and taxpayer. Even with such a kickoff, a mere year later, the newspaper would charge, "The Chamber of Commerce was the deadest organization in which they have ever heard."

In 1926, an alternate to the chamber was formed: the Manhattan Beach Boosters. The group was determined to "put Manhattan Beach on the map as one of the outstanding cities in the Santa Monica Bay" area. More than fifty residents were members. To further advertise the city, the citizenry voted to tax themselves 10 cents for every $100 valuation to be used to promote the city.

Publicity man Morton MaeCormac was hired. He was the secretary of the "new" chamber of commerce formed in 1927, which was actually an arm of the city council. MaeCormac was on the road more then he was in Manhattan, and after his first year, some citizens began to question his frequent absences. He served for only two years.

Progress in the 1920s

With the construction of the Manhattan Beach Pier extension completed, Captain Larsen arrived to begin fishing operations from his barge, the *Georgina*. The barge, converted from a pleasure vessel, became anchored offshore from Manhattan Beach, previously anchored in the San Pedro Harbor. For the next eight years, Captain Larsen operated the barge, as well as managed the pier extension title to the city.

Some of the largest fish were caught off the pier and from the barge. Catching black sea bass that weighed two hundred to six hundred pounds

The forty-five-foot bait boat *Manhattan* served as a water taxi between the Manhattan Pier and the fishing barge *Georgiana*.

was not uncommon. During the Great Depression, many people obtained their evening meals from the sea.

As the 1920s were coming to an end, the community was concerned with the Manhattan Avenue debate, which had started in 1925. The city council approved the linking of the north and south sections of Manhattan Avenue, bringing traffic directly to downtown business establishments. Residents of the north end of the city, who felt they were being asked to pay for something that would benefit only downtown business, formed the Taxpayers League to oppose the measure. They also fought the assessment for a new park now known as Bruce's Beach. Though minorities were not readily accepted in the community, the school system remained integrated. This was unusual for the times.

A straw vote was held on the proposal to link Manhattan Avenue. Faced with 393 against and only 283 voting for the connecting of the two sections, the council rescinded the Manhattan Avenue action, and all plans were halted. The Taxpayers League asked for a recall of the trustees, on the grounds that they were "inefficient, extravagant and incompetent." On February 15, 1927, with help from the Support the Trustees Club, all survived. However, the park plans moved forward.

In June 1927, in the middle of this controversy, the city rejoiced when Proutyline Products started to build its new location in Manhattan Beach. T.C. Prouty, who had opened the company in Hermosa Beach, manufactured architectural tiles. The products were based on his patent for a talc-body tile, which utilized his patented tunnel kiln. One of the divisions in the company was to become Metlox (abbreviation of metal-oxide). This new procedure, which he had invented, adhered metal to tile. The company would employ hundreds of workers and, for many years, was the only factory in the city.

In addition to new businesses, the need for additional school facilities became apparent. Additional classrooms, a kindergarten, an auditorium and a new cafeteria were added to the Center Street School complex.

The decade was coming to a close with progressive ideas. Already the monopoly of the Pacific Electric was threatened with the opening of the Inglewood-to-Manhattan bus line, and automobile transportation was getting attention from the Sepulveda Through Committee, which was trying to open Sepulveda Boulevard beyond Rosecrans Avenue into El Segundo. The South Bay cities were talking about the consolidation of Hermosa, Manhattan and Redondo Beaches. It never happened, for the consolidation committees could not decide on a name to make all three cities happy. The citizens of Manhattan Beach joined with the rest of America in 1928 to give the Republican Party a ringing vote of confidence. The voters in Manhattan Beach cast 558 votes, more than 70 percent of the city's total, for Herbert Hoover, the GOP nominee, and only 222 for his Democratic opponent, Governor Alfred E. Smith.

Crimes Include Bootlegging

Gone were the days of the pioneer; the town was ready to become a city! Clarence E. Jenkins, who had been elected city clerk, had lumber hauled through the sand in order to build a fine home at Highland and Sixteenth Street, where he, his wife and young son lived. Jenkins became the founding president of the Sea Lions Club, the first men's club in the city. He and his wife were known for giving the most beautiful parties in the entire countryside. Permanent and weekend homes were being built, such as the Hartwell retreat, on Manhattan Avenue and Twenty-ninth Street; the C.R. Fisher cottage, on Sixteenth Street near the Speedway (now The Strand); and the W.A. Wilson bungalow at Thirteenth and Manhattan Avenue.

Little is known about the early criminal events in town, but when Marshal Fred W. Petway, the first appointed marshal who served the community from 1912 to 1915, needed additional manpower, he would deputize the number of men needed. If someone needed to go to jail, he had to travel by wagon to the jail in Redondo Beach. In the span from 1912 to 1924, the town would see three city marshals.

In 1929 and 1930, during the Depression, one of the biggest problems for the police was the crowd of visitors to the summer beach activities. Parking problems necessitated the hiring of more parking patrol officers.

In 1917, with the construction of the town's first city hall, located at the corner of Fifteenth Street and Highland Avenue, the police department occupied one small room and a cell on the second floor. The all-volunteer fire department also moved into the city hall. In 1924, the city hired the first regular fireman and paid fire chief, Harry Hicks. The chief and his wife lived in an apartment over the station in the city hall.

Police calls were received and relayed to the officer on duty by the fireman, who also worked twenty-four-hour shifts. When an arrest was made at night, the officer would awaken the fireman on duty and wait while he dressed to come upstairs to book the prisoner.

While parents were admonished to keep an eye on their children, the police were watching out for bootleggers, under the cry, "The U.S. may be dry, but Manhattan Beach is not." In February 1921, Marshal Kukn joined officers from Redondo Beach and Hermosa Beach in a raid on two bootleg joints.

The first raid in Standard Park on Rosecrans Avenue netted nearly $2,000 worth of liquor and sent two bootleggers to jail. The second operation was a little fancier, as the officers sent two men with marked ten-dollar bills to a home on Ninth and Dianthus to buy booze. They exchanged the money for liquor, and the bootleggers exchanged the money for two free nights lodging in jail. These were the first of many operations and presaged a big political bootleg scandal in the mid-1920s.

More information on the town's police department can be found in Jan's title, *Manhattan Beach Police Department*, at Barnes and Noble.

T.C. PROUTY AND METLOX

In the late 1920s, more and more women were seen in the workplace and one of the largest businesses employing women in Manhattan Beach was the Metlox Manufacturing Company. Established in 1927 at the corner of Valley Drive and Manhattan Beach Boulevard, its products were the world-famous Poppy Trail pottery, fine figurines and other types of decorative motifs.

Many young ladies had summer work at the plant, while women like Mrs. Charlotte Rusth, who has lived in Manhattan Beach all her life, had permanent work. With artistic talent and a steady hand, she painted the finishing colors on many of the Metlox designs.

The landscape in 1927 of the first Poutryline Products Company development, looking south on Manhattan Beach Boulevard from Morningside Drive on the west and Valley Drive on the east. The site later became known as the Metlox Company and today as the Metlox Center. Note lack of development in the Hill section.

One of the most well known four acres of property in the city was brought to the attention of residents when T.C. Prouty was searching for a new factory site. The Santa Fe Railway Company had leveled the acreage in 1921–22, intending to build a warehouse and waiting room for its rail line. The construction never took place. However, it is now the location of the Metlox Center. The Proutyline Products Company was founded in 1921 by T.C. Prouty, who was an inventor, manufacturer and visionary. He had been manufacturing architectural tiles in Hermosa Beach before selling the operation to the American Encaustic Tile Company.

By the time he purchased the land in Manhattan Beach, Prouty had several factories around the country and employed over six thousand people. On June 16, 1927, with the groundbreaking ceremony in Manhattan Beach, a new industrial site was launched in the city.

The office/experimental laboratory was the first structure to be constructed. Mr. Prouty had a strong feeling that the South Bay was to become one of the greatest manufacturing districts in the United States, with the Atchison, Topeka and Santa Fe right-of-way corridor developing into an industrial area.

A Santa Fe railroad spur had been laid beside the property, making it possible in October 1927 for the first carload of clay to arrive at the Prouty plant. Clay was one of the ingredients in manufacturing the Metlox non-fading display tile letters. Neon gas letters were placed on tile letters, making it possible for the sign to be seen both day and night. The new technology of neon light combined with glazed tile work brought an unusual beauty and distinctive appearance.

In 1929, Mr. Prouty's sons, Kenneth and Willis, created the Metlox Corporation, which rapidly became the most successful manufacturer of neon signs across the country. The sign company was a subsidiary of the Proutyline Products Company.

As business increased and more workers were employed, another building, the first of its kind on the West Coast, was constructed. The structure consisted of a 50- by 150-foot, all-steel, electrically welded skeleton framework, which was covered with a concrete outer skin. Having the appearance of a Quonset hut, the roof was arched and also covered with concrete slabs. Other buildings housed a machine and metalworking shop, space for expensive machinery used in the manufacturing of Meltox signs and a storage area for steel and other metals. A drafting building, shipping room and sculpturing and molding area in the tile department were also constructed.

In the summer of 1932, the entire plant was reconfigured to suit these changes, and several new smaller buildings were added.

As the Depression approached, the demand for the sign letters began to wear off, and those who had ordered signs bought with credit found they could not pay the bills. To survive the Depression, the Metlox plant began producing three lines of clay dinnerware. One design, "Mission Bell," was created exclusively for Sears & Roebuck Company. The most famous of the lines was Poppy Trail, which received its name from a book of California wildflowers, *California Poppy Trails*, by Evelyn White. The dishes came in a spectrum of colors from delphinium blue to poppy orange, all of which were finished in a high gloss. Material about Metlox is abridged from *Shadows on the Dunes* and *Walk Beside the Sea*, both authored by Jan Dennis.

The Great Depression came late to California compared to the rest of the nation. However, many women saw their husbands out of work, causing the ladies to seek employment.

OIL FRENZY

From the time of the mission era, petroleum was known to exist in the Southern California subsoil. Tar from submarine seepage was a nuisance on the beach. In 1859, George S. Gilbert, a whale oil merchant, distilled semiliquid asphaltum, kerosene and lubricating oil from oil seepage in Ventura County. In 1861, the first documented oil well in the Golden State was drilled near the present hamlet of Petrolia in Humboldt County.

The oil frenzy of the South Bay in the 1920s started with the discovery of the reserves at Huntington Beach in 1920 and at Signal Hill in 1921. In 1921, Redondo Oil Company was already drilling and offering shares for a single dollar. Interest in Manhattan Beach exploration was first raised publicly in 1923, and on September 5, 1824, Consolidated Mutual Oil leased the first land in town for oil drilling.

The first oil drilling took place on George Martin's property, the site of the old Duncan Ranch. Natural gas was found, and Shell Oil bought the land. Manhattan Pacific Oil Company's number two well was drilled and abandoned because of water seepage, but it was later reopened when oil was found oozing between the cap and casing. A third well was begun in 1926 at Pine Street and Marine Avenue, with Bardeen Oil Company drilling a well in the same vicinity.

Three months later, a fourth Manhattan Beach well was established in the Martin Ranch at Gould Avenue and Camino Real (now Sepulveda Boulevard). Martin set up a deal with the Midway Company that transferred twenty-five acres to wildcatter G.W. Johnson of Signal Hill. A wildcatter is a person who develops oil wells in unproved territory.

The drilling activity spurred "property owners, lease hounds, speculators, real estate operators, sightseers and representatives of various oil companies to come to the well," according to the local newspaper. With all the excitement, the City of Manhattan Beach established a new tax of $200 per well and extended the area zoned for drilling to include Second to Seventh Streets between Ingleside Avenue and the Santa Fe tracks.

There were big debates about drilling near the city's water supply, causing many residents to urge a ban on oil production within a five-hundred-foot radius of the city's water wells. At the end of October 1926, the Bardeen well was the last well in Manhattan Beach to close. The city briefly mourned the end of its oil bonanza but was soon over it.

By 1927, the city began to closely regulate beach activities. It introduced an ordinance forbidding ocean swimming beyond four hundred feet from the mean high tide line. By July 1928, city fathers decided there were to be no more bonfires on the beach. However, this did not stop some people from roasting wieners in the "no man's land" between Hermosa and Manhattan. Fishing and swimming were extremely popular. By 1928, to make fishing even better, the city pier was extended at virtually no cost to the city.

Chapter 3
1930s

Depression Era

As the residents of Manhattan Beach headed into the 1930s, there were newspaper stories about recent millionaires jumping from office windows to provide their families with insurance money. The severity of the stock market crash inflicted hardships all around the country. However, it was hard to relate that to the welfare of the middle-class merchants in town and their customers.

Mr. W.B. Carer opened his new Virginian Café at 2404 The Strand, featuring old-fashioned Southern cooking; a tea garden at 313 Eighth Street was opened; and Ruby Warwick opened the first city beauty salon, located in the rear of the Center Pharmacy at the corner of Manhattan Avenue and Manhattan Beach Boulevard. Zahn's Drive-in Market at 3307 Highland Avenue was the first to accommodate car owners by developing parking on sight, and Standard Oil Company, later to become Chevron, was operating new garage and service stations.

As 1930 moved through summer and into fall, the rosy economic promise of the new year seemed to recede. Although employment statistics were not yet kept, it was apparent that unemployment was growing across the country, as well as in Manhattan Beach. In 1922, the State Bank of Manhattan Avenue had been started by A.P. Manning of South Pasadena. Finding the coastal climate unhealthy, he sold his bank interest. The bank was sold, and by October 1931, the State Bank of Manhattan was in trouble. The new

During the Depression, hundreds of people found relaxation and escape from everyday problems while fishing or just strolling on the Manhattan Beach Pier. This view looks west from the bridge at Sepulveda Boulevard and Valley Drive prior to the Santa Fe Railroad tracks, which were laid in 1888, being dismantled.

owners closed its doors for good, unable to honor its accounts. In February 1932, it began paying 35 percent of the deposit value of savings accounts and 30 percent of commercial accounts.

Depositors, as well as those connected with the bank in an official capacity, were surprised by the closing. A citizen's committee was formed to try to save the bank, but the effort was discouraged by the State Banking Department. They felt with troubled banks all over the state, only the more viable ones could be saved.

Manhattan Beach would not have another bank until February 1934, when the Bank of America established a branch in the old State Bank of Manhattan building. As the economy declined, the conventional wisdom advised that the only thing to do was to hold tight and wait it out, and that is exactly what the residents did.

Residents in town mobilized to help their less fortunate neighbors through organizations such as the Sea Lions, the Neptunian Woman's Club, the Manhattan Beach Exchange and the Exchange Welfare Committee. The *Manhattan News* sold old newspapers to help the parent-teacher association buy milk for school children, the city hall employees sponsored Thanksgiving dinner for needy children and the fire department solicited and repaired old toys, making it possible for needy children to unwrap gifts on Christmas morning.

With money scarce and the city's own revenues diminishing almost to the vanishing point, the city government in the spring of 1932 cut its employees' salaries by 10 percent. In July, street lighting expenses were reduced by $3,000. Citizens had trouble meeting their property tax bills, so in 1933, the city approved a moratorium on tax payments, but with the city's own revenue needs, that approach was limited. By the late 1930s, the city was seizing and selling property that had tax delinquencies dating back to the beginning of the Depression.

Political Turmoil

Over the years, several attempts had been made to recall various board of trustee members. By 1926, the name of the city's governing body (board of trustees) had been changed when the state adopted legislation identifying all city lawmaking bodies as city councils. In January 1931, the Taxpayers Protection Association was seeking a recall of two city council members. It was a month later that the recall was voted down, and John F. Jones and Carl D. Edwards remained on the council.

In the meantime, while the petition was being circulated, the entire planning commission resigned because its proposed zoning changes were rejected by the city council. The planning commission had been created by an ordinance in 1928, defining its powers, duties and conduct. By 1932, the original ordinance was repealed and a new commission was recreated.

The early 1930s was a time of turmoil, and there was more to come. The voters were looking for a "strongman" to emerge on the city council, and that man was Rudolph F. Wedler, who was first elected in April 1934. He was the former president of the Taxpayer's League and head of the North End group that opposed projects endorsed by the central merchants and the connecting of North and South Manhattan Avenue.

Mr. Wedler was appointed mayor in June 1934 with the goal of cleaning house in virtually all departments. He attempted to control patronage and job appointments and was quoted as saying, "There is a need to give others who have been out of work an opportunity to share in the city expenditures."

Several departments saw resignations: the fire chief, who had been chief for five years and was a very progressive leader in the development of the department, was forced to resign; another resignation was the superintendent of the Water Department, who had held the office for

In 1933, the first freestanding post office was built by E.L. Nollac, of Los Angeles, located at 1006 Manhattan Avenue. Nollac leased the building to the United States government for ten years.

only two months; and in the fall, the mayor charged the police chief with insubordination. A week earlier, Wedler had charged Chief Haddock with "police laxity" for failing to kill a rabid dog quickly enough. The mayor asked for the chief's demotion to officer but had a difficult time convincing the council to approve his motion. By September 1934, there was a new chief: E.A. West.

Chief West was a well-known lawman, who in 1912, had joined the Los Angeles Police Department as a patrolman. For several years, he served as a traffic officer, plainclothes man and detective. After resigning and going into business, he returned to police work in 1924 and became the police chief of Compton, serving there until 1932. Coming to Manhattan Beach, he resigned after one year, because of "political meddling." Within a period of five years, three police chiefs resigned.

Throughout the Depression years, there was a great deal of discord over various issues in city hall, but Wedler's power slowly declined. He ran the council meetings and city hall until he was unseated as mayor, but he remained on the council until the late '30s and was heavily involved in the city politics through the '40s.

In 1933, with all the controversy at the city council level, the Manhattan Beach Bathing Suit Ordinance was modified by a 4–1 city council vote. Men were now allowed to sport bathing trunks on the beach, and women could now wear two-piece bathing suits, but everyone had to cover up if they were to walk on the pier, The Strand or anywhere else in town.

Movies and Radio

The early Depression of the 1930s ravaged America. Many people escaped their troubles by going to the movies. The motion picture industry boomed with actresses and actors like Jackie Coogan, William Haines, Lila Lee and James Kirkwood Jr. to name a few, all who had a connection to Manhattan Beach. While other construction had stopped or slowed down, new movie theaters were still going up. Metlox, a division of the Proutyline Products Company, was also expanding, building signs not only for the Pantages Theater but also for the Pathe Studio, as well as the Warner Brothers theater in Huntington Park. In 1932, the company signed a contract to sell neon signs in eleven Western states.

While prices were low—a loaf of bread was 7 cents, a gallon of gas was 10 cents, a gallon of milk was 43 cents and gold per ounce was $2.67—many residents were without an income. Like the movies, domestic commercial radio blossomed as an entertainment medium. Manhattan Beach families gathered around their radios throughout the decade to listen to *Jack Benny*, *Fibber McGee and Molly*, *Gangbusters* and many other favorites. Housewives listened to *Ma Perkins* and *Our Gal Sunday*. Kids came home from school and tuned in to *Jack Armstrong*, *The All-American Boy* or *The Lone Ranger*.

In 1932, residents were also introduced to another form of radio service. Mackay Radio Corporation established a relay station at the southwest corner of Sixth Street and Rowell Avenue. The one-story, $1,250 facility transmitted and received ship-to-shore International Morse Code signals for maritime radio communications.

Broadcast fans were already talking about picture radio. A television demonstration was put on as a benefit for the Manhattan Beach Community Church, with tickets being sold in local stores. An audience gathered in the school auditorium, where they saw a sixty-line picture projected onto a two-foot screen.

Edwin Wilson of Los Angeles, who presented the demonstration, noted that while there was no television in the West, some thirty-two stations had been licensed in the East for experimental, non-commercial, non-scheduled broadcasts. He blamed the lack of Western television on the successful efforts of Eastern interests to dominate the new medium.

Not only was there discord in the television industry but there was also bickering here in Manhattan Beach between political factions. A petition on the issue of zoning was being circulated by the Taxpayers Protection Association. They were also seeking a recall and demanding the election of successors for two city council members.

BATHING SUITS AND OTHER CONTROVERSY

The Manhattan Beach Police Department had its hands full with twenty-five thousand people celebrating the wonderful summer beach weather and great fishing. However, there was also another problem. Hermosa Beach was the first South Bay city in early July 1931 to reform the bathing suit ordinance. Children under twelve years of age were not allowed to wear just bathing suit trunks. Two weeks later, Manhattan Beach police chief Alex Haddock was still arresting bathers for wearing their bathing suits in "any other manner than conventionally."

Beach-goers here in town were still wearing the traditional full wool bathing attire. The Manhattan Beach bathing dress ordinance, No. 368, was modified in 1933. Men now were allowed to sport bathing trunks on the beach, and women could wear two-piece bathing suits. Many businessmen opposed the new ordinance but finally were convinced by county officials that they would never prohibit men from wearing bathing trunks. However, everyone had to cover up if walking on the pier or The Strand.

In 1934, the city council exerted firm control over the operation of the police department and Chief Haddock. Mayor Wedler charged him with "police laxity" of failing to kill a rabid dog quickly enough. The chief said that very effort had been made to investigate the case as reported to his officers and himself.

Problems had been brewing for some time between the chief and Mayor Wedler. Another issue the chief faced was the mayor's opposition to the employment of an extra officer. While the chief was on a business trip, the council fired Stanley Hall, a special duty officer. Chief Haddock had put

A cartoon appearing in *Manhattan Beach News* depicting the attitude of the new bathing suit ordinance.

Hall on the police roster after consulting with the police commissioner, as well as several of the council members.

The explanation for the additional patrol officer was due to the recent thefts of plumbing fixtures and numerous other items from properties in the area of Blanch Road, Alma and the pier. The area was to be patrolled three nights a week. However, the mayor felt it was the chief's responsibility to pay the officer's salary out of his own pocket. Chief Haddock refused to pay and was asked to resign because of insubordination. However, by mid-September

Left to right: C. Whitehead (P), R.H. Swain (F), H.G. Sights (P), J. Root (F), Chief A. Haddock. During his tenure as police chief, Haddock held the position of president of the Fire and Police Association. This photograph is from 1934.

1934, the mayor succeeded in getting the council to demote Haddock back to officer status. The friction between the two men soon ended when, in November, Chief Haddock was dismissed from the police force on charges presented by the mayor.

Police files and records were practically nonexistent during this time. However, we do know during that year there were forty-seven arrests and thirty-six parking tickets issued.

Little attention was given to the education of officers. They acquired their police professional trading through the trial and error method and by studying the penal code, as well as the Vehicle Act.

FEDERAL PROJECTS

During the 1930s, the federal relief programs, such as the Federal Emergency Relief Administration (FERA) and the Works Progress Administration (WPA), went into operation. The distribution of surplus food and work projects took

After its development in 1932, Live Oak Park showed large banana trees, which were gifts from the city of Inglewood, California.

place. Not everyone in Manhattan Beach applauded these efforts. Some merchants charged that direct government distribution of flour, beans, clothing and other goods took away their customers for those items.

Putting men back to work was handled by the WPA and the Unemployment Relief Program of Los Angeles County. The county felt that not only did the individual receive help, but the money spent did its bit toward the general economic ability of the community. It was also felt that the work project eventually would enhance property values.

Hundreds of unemployed men worked on various projects, such as road work at Twenty-first Street and Railroad Drive, now Ardmore Avenue; Live Oak Park; tennis courts at the rear of the old city hall; sidewalk construction; the police pistol range, located at Blanche Road and Twenty-seventh Street; Grandview Elementary School; and the city sewer system. Los Angeles County provided money for the widening of Center Street, now Manhattan Beach Boulevard, Highland Avenue and Rosecrans Avenue. By January 1933, seventy families had received a total of $2,963.80 for work done on county projects. In 1934, the State of California would provide employment by improving Gould Lane, the boundary between Manhattan and Hermosa Beach, one of the original roads in the area.

Tennis courts built by the WPA in 1933 were located on what is now the police and fire station parking lot on Fifteenth Street. In the same year, the building (middle ground) was the original Boy Scout House.

Both the pistol range and Live Oak Park were located on land that had belonged to Mr. George Peck. Live Oak Park's five acres had been donated to the city by Peck several years earlier. The park, once the site of a trash disposal dump, was originally built by the county with federal relief funds. In order to fill in the ravine to make the area level, twenty-six registered unemployed men made hundreds of trips back and forth along plank runways moving cubic yards of dirt at a development cost of $14,896. The WPA completed the development and added tennis courts and other facilities.

The park was named for the fifty live oaks that were planted December 9, 1932. The trees stood along both sides of what is now Ardmore Drive, in two groves at the north and south ends of the park. Live oaks were chosen because of their durability in a coastal climate. Many other plants and trees were donated by individuals and organizations, such as the People's Building and Loan of Inglewood.

Sepulveda Boulevard

A thread that ran through the tapestry of Manhattan Beach divided the community both philosophically and physically. The road, once just a dirt path, was lined with eucalyptus trees, planted by the Los Angeles Board of Supervisors as windbreakers from the blowing sand. As it does today, the road, which became the Coast Highway and later Route 1, served travelers moving along the coastline.

Here in town, the thread stretched from the southern border at Artesia Boulevard to Rosecrans Avenue at the north. Once referred to as Camino Real, the path was not part of the original El Camino Real, the "Kings Highway." It had branched off from the original highway, which ran inland, connecting the established twenty-one Spanish missions.

In the early days of development, the area west of the highway saw most of the summer homes and business, while to the east, then known as the "back county," sat the farms, ranches and orchards. For many years, car

In 1934, looking south at the intersection of Sepulveda Boulevard and what is now Manhattan Beach Boulevard. The identification sign was built by the Metlox Company with the arrow pointing to downtown.

bumper stickers read "No Life East of Sepulveda," and real estate agents suggested not buying east of the highway.

The name "Sepulveda" refers to the family and heirs of Jose Dolores Sepulveda, a young Spanish officer who fought for Mexico in the revolution and, in 1822, was sent to Los Angeles as commander of the garrison. He purchased a quantity of horses and cattle and received permission to keep them on a portion of Rancho San Pedro. Before the year was out, he was asked to remove the eight hundred head of cattle from the rancho. Sepulveda refused—in fact, he laid claim to the land and called it Rancho Los Palos Verdes. However, it would be another twenty years before the Sepulveda family was granted an official claim to the rancho. It would be left to Jose Dolores's offspring to develop the rancho since, while traveling back from Monterey, he was caught and killed by Native Americans.

In 1839, another member of that clan, Francisco Sepulveda, had been granted thirty-three thousand acres, which became Rancho San Vicente—land that eventually became part of Santa Monica. The family was extremely wealthy, and in 1852, Don Jose Andres Sepulveda, one of the great landowners of the area, liked gambling. One of his adventures in the sport of horse racing came when he collected five thousand pesos and one thousand head of cattle for a bet on a race. It was perhaps the biggest horse bet that had been made in North America to that time.

View looking southwest to Rosecrans Avenue along Highland Avenue in El Porto. Once an unincorporated community, it is now part of the city of Manhattan Beach.

Having an abbreviated insight into the historical background of the name "Sepulveda" leads us to the development and naming of the boulevard. In 1921, the Manhattan Beach Board of Trustees discussed the figures for an overpass crossing of the Santa Fe Railroad tracks near Valley Drive and the improvement of the Camino Real.

In 1922, Mrs. Wescott opened a hardware store at 218 Camino Real. It was the first to be placed on the southern end of this famous highway at the beach. With more and more travel on the highway, the condition of Camino Real in certain spots developed deep ruts, due to it still being a dirt road. Rosecrans also remained unpaved. It was imperative that improvements be made.

By May 1930, work moved rapidly on the sub-grading, and by October of the same year, the paving of the street was well underway. The most difficult section of the project was the deep grades and necessary cuts through the hill at the intersection of the road and the Santa Fe Railroad tracks. The state built cement piers to support the bridge over the Santa Fe Railroad tracks after bulldozers moved huge quantities of dirt to raise the level of the grade separation over the tracks. The Kuhn Brothers had secured the contract for the construction of the bridge, which called for approximately 1,200 yards of cement.

By April 1931, the work was finished and the strip of highway was open for travel. However, it would not be until 1934 that one could drive north without detouring at Rosecrans Avenue. Not until 1934 was the highway completed through El Segundo.

On October 20, 1932, the stretch of paved highway from Rosecrans Avenue to the southerly boundary was officially named Sepulveda Boulevard by order of the Manhattan Beach City Council when it adopted Ordinance 389.

Police Chief Henry Sights

With the resignation in 1935 of Police Chief E.A. West, Henry Sights, who had served the police department since 1930, became the new chief. The chief had his hands full with car accidents, drunk driving and disturbances of the peace. Records for the fiscal year 1936–37 showed that the police had 4,791 calls, 2,048 arrests, 923 traffic violations and 142 drunk drivers.

Transients invading houses left vacant during the winter months was a continuing problem. Homeowners often returned to their summer homes to find the properties had been vandalized and left in disrepair.

Like his predecessor, Chief Sights inherited a two-patrolmen department, but he started to reorganize. He appointed six new patrolmen, installed the first fingerprint card machine, built a darkroom and issued the first bicycle license. The two patrol cars were outfitted with first aid kits, fire extinguishers, highway flares and radio receiving sets tuned to the Los Angeles frequency.

Cracking down on speeding through town was taken very seriously by the police, and child star Jackie Coogan learned this the hard way. He was given a citation for going sixty miles per hour in a forty-five-mile-per-hour zone. After missing several hearings, he appeared before the city judge, pleaded guilty and paid a fifteen dollar fine.

At this time, several Hollywood personalities lived in or visited Manhattan Beach and El Porto. El Porto, located just north of the town's border, had been subdivided in 1911 and was under the jurisdiction of the sheriff's department. This unincorporated community boasted many celebrities and had its own newspaper column in the *Manhattan Beach News*.

Brooks Barnes reported in the local El Porto column that Sheriff Gene Biscailuz had picked two of his top men to patrol the area. One was former movie star Tom O'Brien, who had starred in the *Big Parade* and quit his $1,500-a-week job over a little misunderstanding with the powers that be. His partner against crime was Al Wolf, who was a master of ragtime piano.

A few weeks later, sheriff's officers, aided by the district attorney's office, raided the El Porto Beach Club located at 3916 Highland Avenue. The club operated on the second floor of an apartment building owned by a Los Angeles Police Department officer.

The club had only been open two weeks when the owner and his two assistants were arrested for taking gambling bets. Owner David Pienna was also charged with suspicion in the shooting of Les Bruneman in Redondo Beach. (Read more about the history and development of the department in *Manhattan Beach Police Department*, by Jan Dennis.)

On the lighter side, film writer Waldemar Young was also profiled in the *Daily News*. It was reported that people were impressed for the way he roller-skated down the steep hill, like *Angel's Flight*, from his El Porto home.

And when Lita Gray Chaplin, former wife of Charlie Chaplin, married Arthur F. Day Jr. at American Martyrs Church, there was no fanfare at the wedding, attended only by her two sons, Charlie and Sidney Chaplin.

The actress had received a church annulment of her marriage to Chaplin, but as the two newlyweds were honeymooning in Avalon, it was found that she had not yet received her civil divorce. The couple was asked to return to Manhattan Beach. After a lawyer and Father Peter Conroy straightened out the mess, the couple were remarried without further problems.

But the ordinary police news and the behavior of the famous was eclipsed on September 26, 1936, by a story that combined both celebrities and mystery. Was it suicide or murder?

The Death of Reid Russell

New Manhattan Beach police chief Henry G. Sight, a native son of Pasadena, California, had served the department since 1929 and was a resident of the town for thirty-five years before his appointment. One of the first things the new chief did was reorganize the department by appointing six new patrol officers.

After one of the desk sergeants, Fireman R.H. Swain, had taken a course in fingerprinting from a mail order correspondence school, Swain was allowed to establish the police department's first records department and fingerprinting/photographic department. In 1936, the first fingerprint card was filed after taking the prints of young African American teenager Willie Wilson.

During the Depression, with more and more people coming into Manhattan Beach to take advantage of the free activities at the beach, a police reserve force was formed. The men usually worked on weekends without pay, issuing parking citations as well as performing regular police duties.

A junior police patrol was also organized, consisting of sixteen young boys of grammar school age. They were instructed by police officers in various elements of police work. The purpose of this instruction was to instill in the youngsters of the community the importance and value of good citizenship and the emphasis of staying away from criminally active youth gangs.

The police department put great emphasis on safety in the community. In 1939, the city received the State Safety Award from the California Traffic Safety Committee. However, speeding traffic tickets, parking citations and the misbehavior of famous people were eclipsed by a story that combined both celebrity and mystery.

On September 26, 1936, an auto salesman named Mr. Reid Russell, twenty-eight, was found shot to death in a garden swing on the Second

Left to right: Lila Lee, actress and former wife of actor James Kirkwood; Gouverneur Morris; Mrs. Morris; and Captain Clyde Plummer, chief of the district attorney's Bureau of Investigation. James Kirkwood Jr. (not shown), while living with the Morrises, attended Redondo Union High School. He went on to become an actor and playwright, winning awards for co-writing *A Chorus Line*. His 1960 book, *There Must Be a Pony*, portrayed the events surrounding the death of Reid Russell.

Street estate rented by famous mystery novelist Gouverneur Morris. The event catapulted the city into the national news world. It was stated that Mrs. Ruth Morris spied the body using binoculars while standing on the upper balcony of the mansion. The body was lying on its back in the swing with a gun in its hand. It was Police Chief Sights who declared, after limited investigation, that it was suicide and closed the case. However, Russell's mother did not believe her son would kill himself and wanted the case reopened. Captain Clyde Plummer, chief of the district attorney's Bureau of Investigation, reopened the case November 13, 1936, on the basis of Mrs. Russell's challenging questions: Where were the discharged gun shells? Why did the gun barrel show no indication of having been fired? Why were Russell's hands washed before a paraffin test was taken?

Captain Plummer believed the death to be a lover's slaying involving Mr. Russell, Mrs. Morris and Ms. Lila Lee. Lila Lee was a screen actress who lived with the Morris family along with her twelve-year-old son, James Kirkwood Jr. But there was another theory. Could Russell have been killed because he knew too much about an international smuggling ring?

Theories in the Russell Case

The newspapers stated that Ruth Morris discovered Russell's body, the deceased clutching a gun in his hand. Mrs. Morris was using her binoculars while standing on the upstairs balcony. Chief Sights declared the incident to be a suicide, despite the fact that there was no gun cartridge casing found in the area, the victim's hands had been washed and there were no notes found.

The case was reopened a month later at the urging of Russell's mother, Victoria, who denied her son would kill himself. She said he was happy the last time she saw him and suspected he had been seeing an older, wealthy woman. Captain Clyde Plummer, chief of the district attorney's Bureau of Investigation, reopened the case November 13 on the basis of Mrs. Russell's

The back of the Morris home showing the upper balcony from which Mrs. Morris observed the body of Reid Russell in the swing. The house (still standing today) was built/owned by Myron Wells in 1933.

charges. The captain believed the death to be a love slaying involving the two women who lived in the house.

However, the Morrises told detectives that Russell had often talked of suicide and that he indeed had left a note with Mrs. Morris. When asked for the note, she said she had burned it thinking that the case was closed, showing it only to Lila Lee.

But there was another theory that Russell may have met his death because he knew too much about an international smuggling ring. This came out after Los Angeles police detective Lieutenant Harry Hannsen told the captain of a conversation the former had with Russell at a wild, two-day party just a few days before Russell's death. This led to suspicion that perhaps Russell did not die on the swing but was carried there after being shot elsewhere. In support of this was the fact that the rusted barrel of the gun held in Russell's hand showed no indication of having been fired.

Headlines changed from calling it suicide to a love slaying, but it ultimately became a mystery and remains so to this day. The case is still open, and investigators have found no new evidence. Interest gradually died down in the case, although it was reopened twice more. Each time, Mrs. Morris was a significant witness.

The Morrises went to live with friends in New Mexico in 1938. A few weeks after arriving, Mrs. Morris, who had gone insane, died. Gouverneur Morris lived until 1953. Lila Lee would go on to do a string of "B" movies until her death in 1974. James Kirkwood Jr., while living with his mother and the Morris family in Manhattan Beach, attended Redondo Beach High School. He went on to become an actor and playwright, winning awards for co-writing *A Chorus Line* and receiving credit for *Some Kind of Hero*. His 1960 book, *There Must Be a Pony*, portrayed the events surrounding the death of Reid Russell. More information on the case can be found in *A Walk Beside the Sea.*

While murder may have occupied the minds of the townspeople for a while, it soon faded from view and the residents once again picked up the forms of recreation they had temporarily put aside.

Aquaplane Race

During the Depression, beach lovers may have felt that the sun, sand and surf were free, but the City of Manhattan Beach knew better. In order to maintain the pier and roundhouse, the city needed funds. In order to receive

Well-known swimming athlete and actress Esther Williams is pictured presenting the winning Aquaplane trophy to Bill Burred.

funds from the county, the Manhattan Beach City Council, in August of 1935, designated the Manhattan Beach Municipal Pier as the continuation of Center Street, now Manhattan Beach Boulevard, with two-thirds of the money going to pay labor. County funds were also used to widen Highland and Rosecrans Avenues, with the work being done by the Works Progress Administration.

Another event in 1935 was regarded as the greatest single sporting event to be held on the California coastline that year. On August 2, 1935, after months of negotiations, Logan Cotton, chairman of the junior chamber of commerce, announced that the stage was set for the grand Aquaplane Race. Some one hundred competitors would stand erect on wide boards while guided by a rope line being pulled behind speedboats often reaching speeds of fifty miles an hour. Each boat consisted of a driver and mechanic.

The 26.6-mile race crossed the channel from Catalina Island to Manhattan–Hermosa Beach. The first race was held in 1935, and by 1937, an estimated 245,000 people gathered on the beach to watch the event. After making the crossing, riders were to leave their boards at a designated spot outside the breaker line and then swim to the beach for the finish line. The public standing along the shoreline could hear the progress of the event from a speaker system furnished by the Standard Oil Company (now Chevron) and Safeway stores.

For the second annual race, a special blue and yellow Aquaplane Race promotional stamp was ordered for use on all city outgoing mail. Design entries were submitted from as far away as Santa Barbara and San Diego. Rader Fink, a young newspaper artist, drew the winning entry.

For years, the event was enormously popular. However, the crowds eventually began to dwindle. The races were interrupted during World War II, and later aquaplanes were replaced by water skis—thus the demise of an exciting sport.

The annual Water Sports Regatta of swimming, paddle boarding and boating, which started in 1927, was held through the 1930s. Another water sport that came to the community in the 1930s was surfing. In 1938, a surfing club was started with the pier as its meeting place. Although thousands of people would flock to see fireworks displays launched from the pier by the Golden State Fireworks Company, hundreds came just to ride the waves.

Another event that people could enjoy was the city float in the Tournament of Roses Parade. In 1915, Manhattan Beach first tried to compete in the parade but failed to find a shelter large enough to house a float during the winter storms. In 1933, it was decided to try again, and by 1934, the city's first entry was complete. The city competed over the next four years and went on to win first place in its class in 1937. A goldfish titled "A Fisherman's Romance" was a thirty-two-foot-long creation made up of orange marigold and yellow pompoms. The eyes were made of shaded delphinium, stevia and maidenhair fern with foam of white narcissus.

In 1938, Manhattan Beach again won honors in the Rose Parade for "Star of the Sea," which took second prize in its class. More than ten thousand blossoms were used on the gigantic starfish.

The decade was coming to an end, and the cloudy skies of the Depression were turning to sunshine.

THE WILLIAM HAINES CASE

There were many personalities living in Manhattan Beach during the '20s and '30s, which brought the community and Chief Sights into international spotlight. One such incident was the despicable treatment of Mr. Bill Haines, a matinee idol in the '20s and '30s at Metro-Goldwyn-Mayer, and Mr. Jimmy Shields, who was Haines's screen stand-in. Haines and Shields spent summers in a rented house located on Moonstone Street in El Porto, where they entertained many of their friends.

It was June 1936, after a day of partying with friends on the sunny beach, when a local six-year-old boy chased and played with a toy poodle belonging to Haines. In the late afternoon, the small boy was given six pennies as a bribe to go home. It was this action, the parent's suspicion and the fact that the men had been targeted for their lifestyle by the White League, the Southern California version of the Ku Klux Klan, that led to the most regrettable scene.

As the dinner guests were leaving the Haines' home, a white-hooded mob appeared, warning them not to come back to the area. The white-hooded mob also splattered the guests and their cars with tomatoes and eggs. Haines and Shields were knocked to the ground, receiving multiple injuries, as did the poodle. Normally, the police department would have come to the aid of the guests and residents, but without explanation, it did not respond.

A molestation case was brought against the two men relating to the small boy and the six pennies, making world news. However, the case was dismissed due to a lack of evidence.

So distraught was Jimmy Shields that he committed suicide, and Bill Haines was released from the movie industry. He aspired to become a world-renowned interior decorator, working for both movie industry members as well as for international personalities. Yet so shaken by the horror of the experience, he was never to adorn a bed with white sheets again. It was Haines who introduced the decorating world to colored bed linens.

The 1930s, with all its intrigue and bickering between the police department and city hall, was to be put to rest, at least for a short time. In 1937, the Works Progress Administration constructed, at a cost of $45,000, a seventeen-foot addition to the north side of the city hall. The police department was now located on the first floor, with jail facilities and garage space for both police and fire apparatus.

During World War II, the community saw not only officers going off to war but also changes in the police and fire departments. The police uniforms were changed to dark blue, and officers' badges were replaced by stars, which took on different designs. The two departments were now separated; no longer did the fireman work the communications desk or book the criminals, nor did the police personnel drive a fire truck. This arrangement created a

By the end of the 1940s, the police force had three patrol cars and two motorcycle officers (referred to by the department as motor officers). Appearing on the left, Officer Bob Carstens, who stood six foot, four inches tall, was one of the motor officers. Chief Sights stands in front of the black patrol car.

burden for Police Chief Sights, as he now had to pull patrolmen out of the field to work the desk. To make matters worse, the postwar population in town was exploding, causing the eleven officers to work around the clock.

DEVELOPMENT AT DEPRESSION'S END

The Depression years were coming to an end, businesses were getting back in the black and it was time to forge ahead. "Improvement" was the key word.

Roads were regraded and resurfaced in order to open up lands for housing tracts. In January 1937, work had started on the construction of twenty-four homes, and there were to be sixty-five to seventy-five homes built between January and October. One tract of homes was located on Third, Fourth and Fifth Streets, between Crest and Ingleside. The community witnessed an increase in new home buyers, pointing out that for the first time in Manhattan Beach's history, few houses were vacant during the

In 1937, the WPA added to the north side of the old city hall to accommodate additional city employers. Beginning of road improvement looking north from Seventeenth Street and Pine Avenue.

winter months. The summer rental rates jumped, and permanent year-round residents finally outnumbered the summer visitors.

As the new and improved roads made the area more accessible, chicken, fox and mink farms in the "back country" (east of Sepulveda Boulevard) were being divided into fifty- by one-hundred-foot lots. The Pacific Land and Title Company purchased many of the small farms that had delinquent taxes.

With the increase in building came problems with encroachments by private property owners onto city property. There were more than 250 cases of illegal private encroachments from fences, retaining walls, house stairs, porches, wrapped driveways, garages and houses. The controversy went on for weeks, and the Manhattan Beach City Council took a hard line. On December 3, 1937, the council drafted an official ordinance stating that all encroachments on city property were to be removed as soon as possible.

Another project welcomed by residents was the seven-hundred-seat La Mar Theatre. In 1937, the Pacific States Theater began construction for the sum of $65,000. The promotion for the facility claimed to have the finest sound equipment available, built by RCA Photophone. The architecture was modernistic/Art Deco with sea motifs, blue ceilings and mirrored walls. The building represented one of the outstanding structures in the state of California.

On July 30, 1938, the theater had its grand opening, with every lady who attended receiving a piece of beautiful pottery. The first double feature was *Three Bind Mice*, with Loretta Young, and *Go Chase Yourself*. Despite being a landmark for many years, with its fifty-foot tower and neon-lighted, angled marquee, the structure met its demise in 1978.

With all the new development in town and much of the good land held in oil leases, the city passed an ordinance in 1939 forbidding any drilling west of Sepulveda. There were restrictions and regulations placed on drilling east of the boulevard as well. A $500 permit fee and a yearly $500 license charge were put into place, with a $300 fine or three months in jail if the new rules were not followed. These rulings effectively ended oil drilling in Manhattan Beach.

Chapter 4
1940s

A Stormy Start

The 1940s started off with a roar! In the early hours of January 9, 1940, Manhattan Beach residents awoke to the new decade with the thrashing of a violent storm, complete with high waves and winds. The storm signaled the beginning of the breakup of the municipal wooden pier extension.

Approximately ninety feet of the extension, built in 1928, was carried away by the heavy surf shortly after 4:00 a.m. Several of the loosened pilings began swinging like battering rams, finally wiping out nearly half of the structure. The portion carried with it a boat landing, the city winch, a gasoline station formerly owned by Standard Oil, a lifeguard dory and numerous small items of fishing gear. The city street crews had tried to free the large timbers that had broken loose, but the seas were too strong.

Another storm in February 1941 swept away the remaining forty feet of the extension. It was uprooted, turned over on its side, carried by heavy winds and strong current and floated to shore almost intact. This event saved the city $1,500 in demolition fees. To this day, portions of the old extension remain on the sea bottom at the end of the present pier.

The landscape was changing rapidly. In 1930, the community had a population of 1,865 residents. By 1940, there were 6,386. Manhattan Beach was one of the fastest-growing cities in the state of California, with a gain of nearly 300 percent since 1920. After nearly twenty years of contracting off and on with the Engineering Services Corporation, it was now time

Pier extension prior to it being destroyed by high surf and strong winds. January 1940.

to hire a city engineer and create a planning commission to oversee local development.

The State Planning Act was adopted in 1929, giving the Manhattan Beach City Council in 1939 the ability to adopt Ordinance No. 482, creating a City Planning Commission. The commission originally consisted of nine members, all voting members. The city engineer, building inspector and a council representative were also members. Later, the council representative was replaced by a citizen-at-large.

The first major task was the preparation and adoption of a zoning ordinance and master plan of land use. In June 1941, the city council adopted Ordinance No. 500, commonly referred to as the Zoning Ordinance. For many residents, the planning commission was the first arena in which they could express their views on a given land issue.

At this time, the powers and duties of the commission were to promote public interest and understanding of the master plan, as well as review use permits, code amendments, zone changes and house construction. Upon review and, in many cases, a public hearing, a report and recommendations were then sent on to the city council for approval or rejection, as is the case today.

In 1948, another change to the organization was the adoption of Ordinance No. 584, creating a seven-member-at-large planning commission. The city engineer and building inspector no longer had votes and served in advisory capacities only.

The first large project for the commission and the Works Progress Administration was the Sever-Fold Civic Improvement Plan, incorporating what is now Live Oak Park, Dorsey Field and Joslyn Center. In 1938, the citizens had voted $142,000 in participating bonds for the $400,000 development, with the remaining funds to be furnished by federal WPA monies. Houses were being bought and demolished or moved to accommodate the civic center development. Five dwellings situated on the site were located at 305 Sixteenth Street (two), 317 Fifteenth, 321 Fifteenth and the Bradbury home at 316 Thirteenth Street. All were moved to other areas in town.

With all the preparation for the proposed Seven-Fold Improvement Plan, the project never materialized. Citizens were unhappy with the Engineering Service Corporation, there was a lack of funds and the WPA had been disbanded because of World War II.

Women's Civic Pride

In Manhattan Beach during the 1930s Depression, women were deeply involved with social welfare activities and the welfare of their fellow neighbors. As the economy declined, government at all levels seemed powerless to slow or halt the downward spiral.

As the city developed slowly, most of the activities and comforts of life were located on the west side of Sepulveda Boulevard, with east of the boulevard basically still consisting of mushroom, rabbit and truck farms, fruit and vegetable gardens and chicken ranches.

Civic pride was strong in the area, and in 1940, Mrs. Barber, along with several other ladies, fought for the improvements of the streets and schools, fire protection and churches. It was Mrs. Modlin who asked the city to change the name of the area then referred to as the "Goat Country" to Manhattan Heights.

After attending several city council meetings, local residents saw little help come to the area. To put more pressure on the city, a civic and educational improvement group was formed. The East Manhattan Beach Woman's Civic Improvement Club, often known as the Manhattan Heights Women's Club, soon learned the council did not recognize the group.

The women could not understand why their part of town was so neglected by the city. Therefore in 1941, with other residents living on the east side of town, the Property Owners' Association was formed. In order to raise money for the building of a clubhouse, the women gave dinners and auctioned off handmade quilts, articles of clothing and toys. Located on Manhattan Beach Boulevard, where the Art Center is now situated, the facility included a small library, toy loan and a playground. On May 9, 1949, as the result of working together, the cornerstone was laid for the community's third elementary school, Manhattan Heights.

After World War II, civic organizations such as the Manhattan Village League and the Liberty Village Woman's Club worked for the betterment of the community. The clubs are no longer in existence, but during their time as active volunteers, their work was outstanding.

Women knew they had contributed to the community's war effort and they had the potential to influence the domestic scene. However, there was little thought given to women in this sleepy seaside community participating in political roles. Suffragists contended that women were equal to men and should enjoy the same political rights. As more and more women across the nation entered into the field of politics, Mrs. Ruth M. Gorman, on April 8, 1952, became the first woman elected to the Manhattan Beach City Council. After serving almost four years and ready to rotate into the mayor's position, she resigned from the council. She never became mayor and later moved to Dallas, Texas, with her husband. It would be twenty years before another woman sat on the council in Manhattan Beach.

A new mood of activism on the local political scene emerged in September 1968, with the organization of the Manhattan Beach League of Women Voters. Mrs. Doris Rosenberg, along with Mrs. N. Greenman and Mrs. T. Hanley, realized a need to acquaint more women with the political process by providing factual non-partisan information, league-sponsored forums and candidate rallies.

During the seventies, Manhattan Beach's neighbors, Hermosa and Redondo Beach, joined the organization and the name was changed to The League of Women Voters of the Beach Cities (LWV of the Beach Cities), reflecting the expanding area. In 1981–82, after the Centinela Valley League was dissolved, its active members also became part of the LWV of the Beach Cities.

"Safest Beach in America"

More and more people realized the excellent quality of life and the pride taken by residents in the community. In a 1941 chamber of commerce slogan contest, the community was promoted as "Manhattan Beach for Home Life and Shore Life." A prior slogan, "Manhattan Beach: the Safest Beach in America," promoted the beach area a prime destination for fishing, sunbathing and surfing.

There was a great deal of attention given to the shoreline, but there was more to land development than the beach area. In January 1940, a debate over the development of the Sepulveda Boulevard corridor occurred between the city council and many property owners, who had formed the Sepulveda Property Owners Association. The group advocated either a business zone for the entire length of the street or no zone at all.

The planning commission had proposed to the council that the two-mile street frontage be zoned residential. However, it would not preclude spot zoning for businesses, providing the businesses concur to certain restrictions as to subject and type of structure. The issue was sent back to the planning commission to ponder. In later years, the entire street frontage would become zoned for business only (C-2 General Commercial).

Corner of Manhattan Beach Boulevard and Manhattan Avenue, looking east on Manhattan Beach Boulevard in the 1940s.

Controversy was put before the city council again. With the continuing growth of the community and the expanding population, it was realized that the city needed a newer and larger dumpsite. Prior to a formal site, trash was placed in a hole and covered with sand, only to find much of the trash uncovered after a bad windstorm. In the 1920s, the largest trash site was located south of Manhattan Beach Boulevard, between Valley Drive and Highland Avenue, behind the Community Church. The good parishioners of the church were instrumental in getting the rubbish site relocated.

Over the years, trash disposal areas had been located in various locations within the city limits. A site developed by the WPA in the 1930s was west of Valley Drive at the southern end of the Dorsey Field. The area was filled in and is now the location of the Josyln Center.

By the spring of 1940, the site located at the end of Twenty-ninth Street in the 500 block was discontinued and a committee appointed to study the problem. For a short time, the rubbish was hauled to a private dump site near Inglewood. However, the forty-dollar-per-day charge at the location was found to be too costly for the city, and the program was disbanded. After an attempt to operate its own trash service, the city elected to have the trash hauled by outside contractors.

The end of an era began on May 12, 1940, with the gradual phasing out of the Pacific Electric Red Cars. Since 1925, the company had lost $30 million in revenue. With the demise of the system, the company ventured into bus transportation. It claimed the bus service offered cheaper service. The new motor coach service provided seventy-four trips, except Sundays and holidays, between Los Angeles and the South Bay. The fifteen new buses had thirty-seven seats with individual lights and reclining seats and ran every half hour.

A year later, the 139 miles of Oceanside tracks were torn up at the rate of a half-mile a day. Residents worried that the right-of-way would become a commercial blemish to The Strand. To avert a situation, the Manhattan Beach City Council ruled that the land, which had been valued at $180,000 in the city limits, could only be for beach use.

The beach was always an issue. The city quickly adopted new ordinances to fend off Neil S. McCarthy's attempt to place barbed wire around that part of the beach, which he owned.

Local McCarthy Controversy

The beach-related controversy between Mr. Neil S. McCarthy and the City of Manhattan Beach went on for years. McCarthy's attempt to put up barbed wire around his beach property, located between First and Thirteenth Streets, was stopped. When three men, one being McCarthy's son, attempted to build a fence around the plot of land, they were thrown into jail. However, McCarthy did succeed in fencing in his beach portion, being made possible by the California Supreme Court.

After the Supreme Court case, McCarthy installed a smooth wire fence around his beach property and charged a penny or a nickel admission to the gated area, much to the community's displeasure. Due to residents' protests, the Manhattan Beach City Council moved to make beach admission charges illegal.

McCarthy had purchased the land in 1938 from James Cortelyou. Unable to sell the property, McCarthy tried unsuccessfully to subdivide the tract of beach into sixty-foot beachfront parcels. The Manhattan Beach Planning Commission in 1943 passed a resolution asking the county to buy the private beach. However, it would take the state until 1956 to agree to the purchase.

This photograph shows two things that no longer exist—the controversial McCarthy fenced-in plot of beach and the Metlox-crafted sign reading "Manhattan Beach." Note the shallow beach.

Eventually, the fence was destroyed by a storm, never to be replaced, and the Manhattan Beach shoreline was truly a public beach for all to enjoy. More can be read about the McCarthy beach in *A Walk Beside the Sea.*

While the beach issues were being resolved, other land east of Sepulveda Boulevard was becoming urbanized. The fox, chicken, mushroom and truck farms were disappearing and the community's population was growing. To enhance living conditions in the area and to seek recognition and representation, the Manhattan Beach Property Owners' Association was formed.

In 1942, the group completed the Soil Section Community Hall, located on the corner of Herrin Street and Manhattan Beach Boulevard. Like a Midwestern barn raising, the hall was built with contributed funds and donated goods and labor.

Among the first demands would be better fire protection and a direct phone line to the fire station, which was located in the city hall on Highland Avenue. It would not be until 1954 when Fire Station Number Two was complete and dedicated, at the cost of $36,000.

Another area east of Sepulveda that had not yet been subdivided into building lots was the $60,000 purchase by the Pacific Title Company as an investment. Prior to World War II, it was thought that the Star Nursery Company was soon to either purchase or lease the property. It was indicated that the soil was particularly adaptable to raising azaleas and special types of trees. Japanese gardeners were in the process of digging wells and putting in poles to string wire fencing around the entire acreage. With the bombing of Pearl Harbor, which brought the United States into World War II, the Japanese American residents of this area were sent to internment camps. There were several locations in the South Bay area established for internment centers.

The property was never developed into a nursery. After the war, the entire acreage was sold to the Manhattan Beach School District for much less than its value. Since Manhattan Beach students were attending Redondo High School at that time, it was determined a high school should be built on part of the property.

As in most cities, the war brought many changes to this community. It was a time of gold stars hanging in windows, rationing, blackout curtains, paint-on stockings and chenille robes.

The World War II Homefront

During World War II, community progress slowed down considerably. Residents were consumed with the war effort, leaving little time, money or materials for the development of the land, schools or homes. Much of the land in the Soil Section, as well as other parts of town, was planted with victory gardens, supplying residents with fresh vegetables and fruit.

If a contractor could get supplies, he had to build rental units for the defense workers, and homeowners had a $200 cap on improvements. The rental shortage was so acute that garages and storage buildings were converted into dwellings for military families and defense workers. This undertaking is one of the reasons for the "bootleg" problem occurring today—the subdividing of living quarters without city permits.

In 1943, due to the lack of housing, the Federal Housing Authority (FHA) approved a subdivision project on a tract composed of twenty acres, located adjoining Gould Lane, one-quarter mile east of Sepulveda Boulevard. The homes were designed to have two bedrooms and 750 square feet of floor space, on a 50- by 135-foot lot. Another FHA project was given the go-ahead in 1944, located in the fifteen-block site on both sides of Marine Avenue between Sepulveda and Pacific Avenue.

However, there was one area of land that was not used by the residents of the town. The United States government had condemned hundreds of lots located east of Ardmore Avenue to Flournoy Road and south to Fourteenth Street, for the duration of the war. Battery E Coastal Artillery, as well as two eight-inch railroad battery guns, occupied the land. The purpose of their arrival was to protect the South Bay coastline.

Battery E arrived in town from New Jersey on Christmas Eve 1941. Approximately one hundred soldiers camped out in Live Oak Park that first night, later putting up orderly tent rows between Eighteenth and Nineteenth Streets on Flournoy Road. Gun No. 1 and Gun No. 2 rolled on a spur track, which came off the Santa Fe Railroad line. In February 1942, the spur and support bunkers were built across the crest of the hill. After the war, the railroad spur was removed with the bunkers being removed in 1949.

The soldiers and dogs patrolled the shore to keep the public off the beach, and they used The Strand as a transport road until trucks demolished two lampposts. The City of Manhattan Beach forbade multi-axle vehicles along the walkway and billed the army $100 for the posts. The military also enforced blackout rules and dim-out headlight regulations.

The residents welcomed the soldiers by opening their homes for a night, weekend or for a home-cooked meal. For entertainment and dances, the troops could go to the local USO, one of the nine victory houses or the Badminton Club. During the war, the Badminton Club had been used by the U.S. Army as a barracks, as well as for dances sponsored by the club members.

A building owned by the Standard Oil Company at Highland Avenue and Center Street (now Manhattan Beach Boulevard) was donated to the USO for a recreation center. Outfitted with easy chairs and tables, the soldiers could write letters, listen to music and play ping-pong. One soldier was quoted in the newspaper as saying, when he sank into an easy chair, "It's been a long time since I sat in an easy chair like that."

The war at home was dominated by the Red Cross, with its first headquarters located at 1100 Manhattan Avenue, later to move to 330 Center Street in 1942. Under the leadership of Maude Withers, the organization made and sent aid packages overseas, as did the Sandy Shores Navy Mothers Club, which was made up of mothers and wives of service men and women.

The war even changed the daily lives of schoolchildren. There were no interscholastic sports due to the rationing of tires, which created a lack of transportation between schools. Plus, there weren't enough boys to form a football team. Physical training with military-type equipment was emphasized for those high school boys not yet in the service.

PEACETIME AND AFTER

With the headlines on August 17, 1945, reading "War Over," 350 Manhattan Beach residents gathered in the heart of town, and all stores closed, but it was not until the following day that the planned celebration took place. After the war, peace, prosperity and acceleration were the spoken words of the day. The country exploded with excitement, new cars, shopping centers and, best of all, television, which came about for most people in 1947. The gas rationing cards were gone, and the women who worked during the war were expected to return to simply being housewives and raising families.

The community population was mushrooming with the servicemen and women coming home, along with many of the GIs who were stationed here in town with Battery E and factory workers who came from other parts of the country to work in the aircraft and shipbuilding industry. The census of 1944 was 9,286, a roughly 45 percent increase from 1940, when the population was 6,398. Restrictions on building materials were lifted, and lumber became more available, making it possible for people to begin building new homes, offices and rental units.

Along with the population boom was a building boom. An all-time building record was broken in 1946 with 384 permits issued in the first six months of the year. Both the City of Manhattan Beach and the Federal Public Housing Authority were working together to develop several sections of land in town.

The city had surveyed and graded for a ten-unit housing project located at Sixteenth Street and Valley Drive, along with a section of Live Oak Park that was not being used. However, in 1946, the project was abandoned by the Federal Public Housing Authority after the Manhattan Beach City Council moved to withdraw from the project. It was felt that the city could not justify the considerable cost relating to its share of the development.

Subdivision projects were being developed all around town. The three-bedroom "tract" home was an ideal style for a young, growing family, both in terms of design and affordability. East of Sepulveda Boulevard was the ideal area, very well suited for such projects. Manhattan Homes Tract, built by the Bowler Construction Company, was bounded by Marine Avenue to the north, Eighteenth Street on the south, Meadows Avenue on the west and Peck Avenue on the east. The subdivision consisted of two hundred homes, estimated to be worth a total of $1.75 million.

Another subdivision, the Manhattan Village Corporation Tract, which contained three hundred homes, was estimated to be valued at $3 million. This fifty-eight-acre tract, estimated to be ready October 1947, was bound by Marine on the north, Manhattan Beach Boulevard on the south, Sepulveda on the west and Meadows on the east.

There were other changes made in the postwar era, such as the first woman appointed as director of the Manhattan Beach Chamber of Commerce, Mrs. Kirk White. She filled the term of Jack Hill, who had resigned. The chamber supported the installation of parking meters in the downtown area and asked for angled parking on Manhattan Avenue. Like today, the chamber requested that business owners have their employees park off the main business streets.

The chamber also supported the name change from Center Street to Manhattan Beach Boulevard. Unanimously recommended to the city council and planning commission, Ordinance 578 confirmed the name change on December 4, 1947. The chamber was instrumental in setting up a committee to look into the possibility of hiring a city manager who would administrate the city's affairs. It was believed that the city had reached the state of growth and development whereby its best interests would be served much more efficiently via a full-time manager rather than through the five city council members. On August 1, 1948, Clifford G. Petrie took office as the first Manhattan Beach city manager. One of his first projects was a town clean-up campaign, which entailed the beautification of the city and the dismantling of the army's powder storage bunkers. With the filling in of the bunkers, the land was ready to be used for home building lots.

The recovery period in town saw one of the biggest transactions in 1946 with the purchase of Metlox's Pottery Company.

POSTWAR EXPANSION

The late 1940s was a time for both large and small projects in the business world, as well as the cultural world. On a bright sunny day in June 1946, Frank Bauer stood on Sepulveda Boulevard at Second Street watching a section of the world's largest flying boat being transported to Long Beach. The *Spruce Goose* had been built in Culver City in a span of seventeen months. The plane threaded its way along back streets, down freeways and along city streets like Sepulveda in Manhattan Beach.

The South Bay Civic Symphony Orchestra made its debut; the Soap Box Derby events were held for boys twelve to fourteen years of age; a swimming pool was built at 1804 Pine Avenue for the young people of the community; and a youth canteen called the Teen Time Club was established in the octagonal building at the end of the pier.

By 1948, according to the returns of the special census taken as of December 2, 1948, Manhattan Beach had a population of 14,641. Of the total, 7,094 were males and 7,547 were females.

With the amount of residents moving higher, burdens were put on city services. Thus, the need for more water was necessary. In September 1949, two additional water wells were dug with a capacity of 1,500 gallons each. Construction of wells had been a major undertaking during the previous ten years. Six additional wells had been incorporated into the city's water system, making a total of twelve wells to handle the water needs. Six of the older wells were abandoned due to saltwater intrusion. A two-million-gallon, reinforced concrete storage reservoir had also been put into commission, holding Colorado River water, which was flooding into the Metropolitan Water District.

Another service was the construction of a new post office, located at 1140–44 Manhattan Avenue. The structure contained an area of 4,800 square feet and was built at a cost of approximately $30,000. Employing forty workers, the new post office was designed by John Paul Jones and constructed by Young and Shoemaker. Jones, Young and Shoemaker were residents of Manhattan Beach and well known in their fields. The new structure opened its door in January 1950.

Things were changing, even the old familiar streets. In July 1949, by way of resolution, West Railroad Drive was changed to Valley Drive, and East Railroad Drive became Ardmore Avenue. Property owners along the divided streets felt that Railroad Drive didn't sound socially acceptable. It was also felt that the two roads had nothing in common. Therefore, they should not both be renamed Valley Drive. Center Street had become Manhattan Beach Boulevard in 1947.

As the 1940s came to an end, architecture was changing, with more demands put on the amenities of the facilities. Nowhere was this more evident than in the development of the new high school. Property once earmarked for a nursery was found to be the only land large enough for a high school site. There were many obstacles left from previous projects that had to be contended with before the high school could be built. Water wells (one estimated to have been seventy-five feet deep), irrigation systems and deep oil shafts had to be removed. Utilities, water and sewer lines had to be installed.

In March 1949, plans were approved for the new Mira Costa Public High School, formally to be known as Manhattan-Hermosa High School. By May that same year, the groundbreaking ceremony took place. The name "Mira Costa," meaning "view of the coast," was submitted by a Redondo Beach High School teacher. South Bay citizens submitted another eighty-five suggestions for names.

The architectural style featured a series of open one-story buildings where classrooms gave access to a grassy area. The open hallways were designed for an airy, uncluttered appearance. Long rows of rectangular-shaped structures formed the first four classroom buildings. Architect Samuel Lunden, well known for his designs of hospitals and a strong believer in sturdy construction, prescribed thick, reinforced concrete and steel walls, while using rows of windows at the upper level of an otherwise blank expanse.

By 1950, Curlett Construction of Long Beach finished construction of the classrooms, locker and shower buildings, a combination assembly/library/

study hall building, an administration building and necessary support buildings. Mira Costa High School opened its doors on August 10, 1950. On September 30, 1950, at 3:00 p.m., the facility was dedicated with Dr. Roy E. Simpson, state superintendent of schools, as the chief speaker. The complex became a four-year high school in 1952.

By the end of the 1940s, building increased at such a pace that the City of Manhattan Beach Building Department was issuing permits for more buildings during a one-month period than it had in an entire year in the past. Building valuations quickly passed the $6 million mark. This was remarkable when one considers that 90 to 95 percent of construction in the city was residential.

EVAN SHAW AND METLOX

The recovery period after World War II saw new office/residential buildings in town—for example, Dr. B. Star's building at 1216 Highland Avenue. The first floor provided for business while the second floor contained living units. In 1946, one of the largest transactions was the purchase of the Prouty family's Metlox Pottery Company by Mr. Evan Shaw. The property sat at the corner of Manhattan Beach Boulevard and Valley Drive with Morningside Drive on the west.

Born in Pennsylvania in 1909, Evan Shaw was one of six children brought up in Ridgefield Park, New Jersey. His excellent athletic ability won him a scholarship to William and Mary College, where he achieved an outstanding record in many sports. He tried out for the 1932 Olympics, which introduced him to California, where he enrolled and worked his way through the University of Southern California (USC). With Shaw's uncanny ability for turning projects into a profitable enterprise, he became involved in ceramic manufacturing.

The first dinnerware pattern produced at Metlox under Shaw's leadership was "California Ivy" under the trade name Poppy Trail. From the very beginning, the company showed a profit. The business was taken out of the red with a $600,000 gross in the first year. Evan Shaw and Metlox were to go on to become world leaders in ceramic dinnerware and artware.

Metlox Pottery was the oldest and largest manufacturer in Manhattan Beach at its height of production. It employed some five hundred people and was the last of the five major American pottery manufacturers. The demise of the facility occurred in 1989, when the entire complex was razed.

An aerial view in the early 1940s of Metlox and the civic center, prior to the building of the previous police and fire departments. The large building to the upper left was the old city hall, which occupied the present city hall location.

As employment and businesses grew, so did the population. Thousands of families were leaving the "Frost Belt" for the sunshine of Southern California. In Manhattan Beach, schools could not be built fast enough to keep up with the increase in student population. Actual school budget for 1947–48 was $248,916 with an average daily student attendance of 1,263. This figure, however, did not take into consideration high school students, who mostly attended Redondo Beach Union High School.

At this time, there were two elementary schools in the Manhattan Beach City School District: Grandview Elementary and Center Street School, which in 1948 provided some of the buildings for Pacific School. With the arrival of Forster A. Begg as the district's new administrative superintendent, the upgrading of the school system began.

The first school to be built east of Sepulveda Boulevard was Manhattan Heights Elementary, located at Sixth and Herrin Streets. In 1946, a $275,000 bond was passed, and plans were approved by 1947. The setting of the cornerstone was celebrated the same year. The school setting was in an extremely rural area consisting of rutty dirt roads, with horse trails and no sidewalks. The area was made up of many ranches and farms. In 1987, it was thought the City of Manhattan Beach would purchase part of the closed school grounds. However, the facility was later razed, with a housing tract replacing the old school site.

In May 1948, another elementary school was dedicated, this time a private school—American Martyr's Elementary. This facility was a dream of Father Edmond O'Donnell, who arranged in 1944 for the parish to buy a plot of several acres on a sand hilltop west of Laurel and Seventeenth Street. At a cost of $150,000, the school was to house 240 students. Over the years, the eight classrooms became inadequate, and several more rooms have been added to handle hundreds of students. The parochial school was staffed by eight Sisters of St. Joseph of Carondelet and two lay teachers. "Manhattan Beach was one of the fastest growing and potentially one of the most attractive small cities in California," according to the *Manhattan Beach News*. As the community continued to grow, so did the need for a high school.

Chapter 5
1950s

Mira Costa's Sixtieth Anniversary

In 1921, a high school had been proposed west of the grammar school on Pacific Avenue, now the location of Pacific Elementary School. However, the facility never materialized, and prior to the construction of Mira Costa High School, many of the Manhattan Beach High School students attended Redondo Beach High.

On May 24, 1949, groundbreaking took place for the first high school in Manhattan Beach. The forty-acre site located north of Gould Lane (now Artesia Boulevard) and west of Peck Avenue had belonged to a Japanese American citizen who had been in the nursery and landscaping business before being interned during World War II. After the war, this trace of land was found to be the only parcel large enough for a high school site. The land had not been earmarked for development, however. Realtors knew the land could sell for $2,000 per acre, making it worth well over the $60,000 the school district paid.

Many obstacles had to be overcome prior to construction. Firstly, the site was miles away from sewer and utility lines. Secondly, the nearest water supply was one-quarter mile away. Thirdly, there were no street facilities adequate for commuters. Lastly, there was a large hole filled with water, estimated to have been seventy-five feet deep, in the center of the site. However, all was solved, and on September 30, 1950, at three o'clock in the afternoon, it was a grand day and a dream come true.

Girls League Executive Board, shown in 1952–53.

Dr. Roy E. Simpson, state superintendent of schools, delivered the formal dedicatory address for the opening of Mira Costa High School. Following Dr. Simpson's remarks, Mr. N.R. Kuhn, president of the board of trustees for the South Bay Union High School District, spoke to the hundreds of residents and friends who attended the ceremony. "The completion and occupation of this new high school is indeed gratifying to the board of trustees of the South Bay Union High School District," he said. "For many residents of Manhattan, Hermosa and North Redondo, the construction of the Mira Costa High School is a dream fulfilled, for they have long sought the development of a high school in the northern end of the school district. These people and many others living in this area rejoice with us today as we assemble here to dedicate these buildings." These remarks appeared in the first copy of *La Vista*, the school newspaper. After the ceremony, visitors were invited to take part in an open-house tour of the new facility.

The name "Mira Costa" has its own history. Two years prior to the completion of the school, citizens, students and teachers submitted over 125 names suitable for the new facility. A teacher at Redondo High School, Mr. Richard Gonzales, submitted the chosen name "Mira Costa." According to the Spanish teacher, Mr. Al Applegate, the words freely translated means "view of the coast."

Little time was lost before the first football pep rally. It took place on September 29, 1950, in the latter part of the lunch period near the library. On October 6, in the library, the school's first night social event took place with a "pep dance" in honor of the football team. The price of admission was a mere fifty cents per couple. Women of the community—especially those who were mothers or high school students—pitched in to raise money for the new public high school. The first meeting of the Mira Costa PTA took place on the night of September 21, 1950, with the election of officers and the introduction of the faculty.

For many years, the PTA, school staff and parents raised funds by presenting plays known as the annual PTA Varieties and PTA Capers. In March 1951, the first play, *Why Teachers Go Nuts*, was co-directed by Mrs.

1956–57 Queen Cecily Bond and King Nick Comites at the Fourth Coronation Ball, held at Mira Costa High School Gymatorium.

Mary Friend and Miss Helen Fowler. In future years, there were titles such as *Leap Year Frolics*; *South Bay Pacific*; *Hooray For Friday*; *Shake, Rattle, Sh-Boom*; *The Big Blast*; and *The Capers of 1957*. The last PTA Capers was *Around the World in 80 Daze*, which took place in 1958.

In December 1952, the Gymatorium opened, serving not only as a multi-purpose facility for boys' and girls' physical education but also as the auditorium for the school. The auditorium we now see was built and dedicated in February 1962.

Over the past sixty years, there have been many improvements to the campus and thousands of students, with joy and tears, experienced a wonderful education. Congratulations to you all!

Fun and Games

The 1950s had a playful air about them, with Miss Manhattan Beach Beauty Contests, all ages surfing the high ocean waves, the first paddleboard races and the first Woman's Open Volleyball Tournaments all taking place in the city. The Manhattan Beach Parks and Recreation Department and the chamber of commerce sponsored the first annual Beach Volleyball Tournaments championship, while combining the event along with the International Paddleboard Festival activities.

Mr. Hal Perry, honorary mayor of Manhattan Beach and the star of the radio show *The Great Gildersleeve*, brought many starlets and actors to the chamber's promotional events. Among the celebrities were Robert Stack, Michael Landon, Jock Mahoney, Shirley Jones, Jennifer Holder and Cathy

A December 1955 Girls League Christmas project at Mira Costa collected 2,344 cans of food and $230.05. Standing around the tree, left to right, are: Jim Green, Verl Cunningham, Gwen Strong, Claudia Rhind and Bill Morse.

Case. More information and photographs about the seaside events can be found in the book *Manhattan Beach Pier* by Jan Dennis, available at the chamber office or Hillside Pharmacy.

Like the area around the municipal pier, the school system was also experiencing an increase in activity. Mira Costa High School, formerly known as Manhattan-Hermosa High School, had opened its doors on August 10, 1950, and became a four-year facility in 1952. Realizing the need for more school space, Pacific Elementary's campus, through the use of bond monies, underwent expansion in 1951, with several more additions over the next decade.

The first Intermediate School Center also would see additional floor space. During the 1950s, there would be five lower grade schools added to the Manhattan Beach School District: Meadow Elementary; Peck Intermediate, later to be renamed Foster A. Begg; Morningside, later to be renamed Robinson Elementary; Aurelia Pennekamp Elementary; and Ladera Elementary.

Three other facilities were built on district property: the administrative offices located at 1212 Laurel Avenue, the maintenance and warehouse building at 1200 Peck Avenue and the community swimming pool located adjacent to the Foster A. Begg Intermediate School. By the end of the 1950s, the district's average daily attendance was 5,343 students.

With the elementary schools expanding, there was a need for additional high school space. On November 11, 1957, a new high school was dedicated in North Redondo Beach. Aviation High School was attended by hundreds of youngsters from Manhattan Beach.

With the city population steadily growing, it became evident that the community had to build: multiple-family residences, more commercial enterprises and small home remodels. All departments kept pace. The Manhattan Beach Police Department, under the command of Chief H. Jerome "Jerry" Withers, had grown 68 percent, from thirty-one employees to fifty-two, and the fire department, under the command of Chief Rothwell H. Swain, enlarged its force by ten, reflecting a 42 percent increase in personnel in 1955.

Early in 1957, the public works department was created, thus putting all public works–related activities under one director. With this reorganization came reduced manpower, which saved the taxpayers more than $1 million in nine years without any service losses or cuts. The massive amount of capital improvements during those years stood out and made the '50s the city's most progressive decade.

New projects were also developed. A second fire station, located on Manhattan Beach Boulevard and Rowell Avenue, was dedicated in 1954. Due to the increase of water usage, a new 7.5-million-gallon water reservoir was constructed on Sixth Street near Rowell Avenue. Roads were graded, curbed, widened and resurfaced, while multi-million-dollar storm drainage systems were installed. Parks were improved, and Polliwog Lake Retention Basin was contained.

Accelerated Growth

The Manhattan Beach population influx continued to increase every year. In 1950, the census recorded a population of 17,330. By 1953, the number grew to 26,315. It was distributed as 12,982 males and 13,333 females, with eight non-white residents—five males and three females.

The Manhattan Beach Police Department was also steadily growing, with additional patrol cars and better communication equipment. With a teletype machine installed in the department, reception and transmission of information could be sent anywhere in Los Angeles County.

The fast growth of the city was accompanied by an accelerated infrastructure, improved transportation routes and a higher standard of living, which created demand for more development.

In 1950, the newest tract showed the trend toward continued development east of Sepulveda Boulevard. The Liberty Village housing tract, named after the project contractors, Liberty Builders, contained seventy-five acres bounded by Redondo Avenue, Aviation Boulevard, Marine Avenue and Manhattan Beach Boulevard. With four hundred proposed homes loosely patterned after the California ranch style and an investment of approximately $4.5 million, the City of Manhattan Beach's previous building permit record was shattered.

By October 5 of the same year, the first family, Mr. and Mrs. Robert Merchant and their son, moved into their new home at 2105 Wendy Way. During that period, twenty additional families moved into the section between Nineteenth and Twenty-third Streets on Wendy Way and Faymont Avenue. The two streets were named in honor of the builder's daughters, Wendy and Fay.

During the same period of time, the Type C armory was still being built when President Harry S. Truman ordered troops to help South Korea, which had been invaded by North Korea. Shortly after the troop participation, the

South Bay mobilized. Again the citizens of the community were in close contact with the military. Citizens became involved with blood drives, first aid classes were scheduled and volunteers were going door-to-door in an effort to raise funds for the Red Cross.

In 1951, upon the dedication of the armory located on Bell Avenue, Companies B, H and S of the 578th Combat Engineer Battalion were stationed at the armory, as well as the National Guard Defense and Security training facility. Prior to this facility, the company had been housed at the Property Owners Association Hall, located on Manhattan Beach Boulevard and Herrin Street. A small contingent of army soldiers were also stationed on a Nike base, which was located at Marine Avenue near Redondo Avenue, now the locations of Marine Park.

Many local families invited the servicemen into their homes for the holidays and weekends. The young servicemen contributed to civic activities by delivering and planting ice-plants along the railroad tracks, helping the Garden Club plant climbing roses donated by Bishop's Nursery on the fence that lined Marine Avenue and helping downtown merchants erect Christmas decorations.

The 1950s were also a time of surf, sand and stars; cleaner beaches; beauty contests; volleyball tournaments; paddleboard races; new schools; and social organizations.

POLICE TECHNOLOGY UPGRADED

During the World War II period, the Manhattan Beach Police patrol cars could only use their parking lights at night due to the fear of submarine scares along the coast. After the war, many of the army personnel stationed here serving in Battery E Fifty-second Coastal Artillery stayed in town. More housing was being built, and the police patrolmen had their hands full with an increase in arrests. The town was small, with a population of approximately 7,000, but officers were arresting more than 1,400 people a year, many of them visitors involved in traffic infractions.

To bring the point of safe driving to the public's attention, Manhattan Beach police chief Henry G. Sights devised the "violation card." This card, with its warning on the front and the poignant poem on the other side, was handed out to violators of every observable traffic offense.

Police Chief Sights understood the need for education and required officers to attend all available schools offering instruction in law enforcement,

Photographed in 1955, Chief Henry G. Sights (center right) and Jerome "Jerry" Withers (center left). The Manhattan Beach Police Department kept pace with a 16 percent increase in population from 1955 to 1965. The department increased personnel from thirty-one to fifty-two employees.

procedures and methods. By 1944, the department had approximately 4,216 criminal record cards on file in the fingerprint classification.

Technology in the field of communication continued to improve by 1950. New radio units were installed in the patrol cars and motorcycles, and the Manhattan Beach Police Department could now talk with seven South Bay cities. Up to this time, the department could only communicate with other departments by telephone, except for the El Segundo Police Department. Manhattan could only talk by radio to that station.

A teletype machine was also installed in the Manhattan Beach Police Department, facilitating the sending or receiving of information from anywhere in Los Angeles County between the hours of 8:00 a.m. and midnight. By 1952, it was possible to receive twenty-four-hour service.

The years 1952 to 1953 were hard for the city's chief of police, from being in a traffic accident while driving a city vehicle, which lead to a $52,400 lawsuit, to being involved in a grand jury probe. The grand jury probe eventually involved the entire police department. Chief Sights was charged with mismanagement of public funds and bribery. After surrendering himself into Los Angeles County Jail, four months later he was acquitted of all charges. By 1954, the chief and the department were exonerated, but things did not settle down.

With more than twenty-five officers—four of which were riding motorcycles—and two detectives, the patrolmen finally received a pay raise to $340 a month. In 1955, they were entitled to seven paid holidays a year, and by 1956, the monthly salary of a police officer was increased to $413. The department also added two lieutenants and a captain, making a force of thirty officers.

The year 1956 was to be another political year for the department. Chief Sights, who had joined the department in 1929, had served twenty-one years and found it time to retire. His assistant, Jerome "Jerry" Withers, was appointed the new chief of police on November 29, 1956.

In 1937, "Jerry" Withers, a native son of Manhattan Beach, joined the department at the age of twenty-seven as a patrolman. When he joined the force, he was one of seven officers serving the city. In 1942, he joined the U.S. Coast Guard and served as a chief gunner's mate in the North Pacific aboard the frigate USS *Albuquerque*.

ARCHITECTURAL STYLE

During the late 1950s and into the 1960s, Manhattan Beach saw a bold and innovative architectural style emerge. The city's building pattern had almost completely changed from the previous years. Having been seen in other parts of the world since the 1920s, the first commercial international style of architecture appeared in Manhattan Beach in 1957.

The corporate international style, which had an appearance of weightlessness and simplicity, found its place in the community. An outstanding example of this international style, designed by Mr. Craig Ellwood, can be seen at the corner of Eighteenth Street and Sepulveda Boulevard. Ellwood was considered to be one of the most outstanding designers in the architectural world.

Except for a smaller store project in 1948, a remodeling for KML Royal Dutch Airlines, the bank building was Ellwood's first commercial design. His trademark became the fluency with which he worked with steel, aluminum

Leaving the tradition of commercial building, this 1965 classic elliptical bank building was created by architect Chancy Miles Lott, AIA.

and glass. He had extensive attention to details, quality of materials and sun control for glass areas.

Other commercial and public buildings portraying this same modern design appeared in such structures as the Joslyn Center, the bank at Artesia and Sepulveda, the original Baber Chevrolet agency and showroom at Eighth Street and Sepulveda, and the old Fifteenth Street Police Station and Fire Station, all built in the mid-1960s.

Although the traditional home was still being built, innovative and dramatic designs were the showcase of the 1960s. The international style for homes had many of the same characteristics as commercial structures. Samples of the modern style of architecture built in this timeframe were reflected in architect Edward H. Ficiett designs, which are still located on The Strand.

The John and Marian Scott home, also on The Strand, was the first steel-framed residence in town. Steel was the material of choice in order to span greater space without the need for interior or exterior supporting walls or posts, thus eliminating the typical need for hallways and isolated cubicle rooms.

Architect John Blanton developed a unique style and philosophy when it came to design, and he designed many homes in the community after arriving in Manhattan Beach in 1964. He became the only architect to appear in the local telephone classified section. At that time, very few homes were designed by a professional architect. More can be read about John Blanton, as well as other architects and builders, in *Shadow on the Dunes, an Architectural History of Manhattan Beach* by Jan Dennis.

In the decade of the 1960s, building permit activities saw the issuance of approximately 1,100 single-family units, 743 multiple units and 2,884 alterations and additions. However, for a short time in 1965, single-family home construction stalled. With the Federal Housing Administration controlling 90 percent of all loans for new home construction, money became very tight and a builder needed 30 percent down to obtain a bank loan. Single-family homes were also being gradually replaced with the construction of apartments, additions to existing buildings and general remodeling.

When financing became more readily available, many landowners requested variances to split their lots due to the lack of land expansion, the increase in population and the demand for new housing.

ADVENT OF POLLIWOG PARK

Overwhelmed by the growth of the community, the City of Manhattan Beach was trying to make new residents welcome. In 1951, the city clerk sent out a letter to all new residents. It read: "Dear —, It is with distinct pleasure that we extend to you a warm and hearty welcome to our 'Friendly City of Homes.' We want you to know that it is our sincere desire to assist and cooperate with you in any way possible to make your residence in Manhattan Beach a pleasant one. Please feel free to call upon us at any time for information or service required…it is our aim to create a friendly and helpful relationship between our city government and its citizens."

In many ways, the city compared its officials to the officers and directors of any large business enterprise anywhere in the country. The main goal was to run that enterprise in an economical and efficient manner and in accordance with the wishes of the majority of the stockholders—in this instance, the citizens of Manhattan Beach.

In the mid-1950s, heavy rain created local flooding hazards along many streets and other areas, prompting residential concern. One such area was the Brown Ranch, now the location of Polliwog Park. "El Rancho de Juez," owned

Looking north from Manhattan Beach Boulevard across what is now Polliwog Park. At the center of the water's edge is Premier Little League baseball field.

by Judge Benjamin Brown, had been a part of the Redondo Land Company when it was subdivided, surveyed and filed for record on September 3, 1897.

The ranch was not only a working ranch with palomino and quarter horses but also a wonderful spot for social events. Powwows attended by athlete Jim Thorpe and Indian tribe leaders were often featured at the ranch. Barn dances were held by Northrop employees. Boy Scouts and Cub Scouts used the facilities, as did Little League players.

With the surrounding areas being built up, developers were given the okay from city engineers to drain onto the Brown Ranch. This placed a major portion of the thirty-acre site under water. After a heavy rain, the pond that was normally only inches deep could swell to four feet. Often one could see boats towing water skiers over the pond. Many residents felt that the pond was a health hazard.

Spearheaded by the Women's Club of Manhattan Beach, local citizens worked to place a bond issue on the ballot in order to purchase the ranch for the purpose of developing a park. The hope was that Los Angeles County would join with the city to create a regional park. However in 1955, the county determined "that the area was not suitable for regional park purposes." The county commission's report stated that "the depression area, even in the future, would appear to limit the usefulness of the site for active recreation purposes."

The Manhattan Beach Unified School District owned eight acres adjacent to the ranch. On July 12, 1956, the district filed condemnation proceedings under eminent domain, requiring the acquisition of the Brown Estate Ranch. After a long court battle, a settlement was reached whereby Mrs. F.T. Brown received $60,000 for the property, an amount lower than the appraiser's value. In later years, the district leased a portion of the property to the city in order to develop Polliwog Park. The park was dedicated in 1976.

Meanwhile, the city's infrastructure was improving and new homes continued to be built, giving residents a chance to enjoy community recreational programs. In 1954 on the old Brown Ranch, Premier Little League was the first baseball organization established for young boys. The city at one time sponsored a baseball program, but that was canceled due to complaints about using taxpayer dollars to subsidize it.

SOIL SECTION

As we look back over the history of Manhattan Beach, we find a great deal of information about the "sand section" west of Sepulveda Boulevard and the downtown area. Abundant with lovely wildflowers and wildlife, such as coyotes, foxes, rabbits, quail and other small animals, the area north of Artesia and south of Manhattan Beach Boulevard was once claimed by farms of various types. The "soil section" was once known as the "back country," and the farms supplied residents with eggs, butter, chickens, rabbits, fresh vegetables, honey and fruit, as well as mushrooms, potatoes, cantaloupe and berries.

Another farmer in the area was James H. Young, who bought the Duncan Ranch east of Sepulveda—and also the highest point in the city, at 245 feet above sea level. Water was suspected to be a mere sixty to sixty-five feet below the surface on the ranch, and Young proposed to sell the water to the City of Manhattan Beach at a rate of six cents per one thousand gallons for fifteen years. However, the city established its own water system, along with other improvements.

By 1923, most of the streets running west to east were renamed to numbered addresses. Gone were names such as Graham, Allegra, Plant, Robinson, Perry, Torrance and Willes, and most of the "back country" was subdivided. However, neighborhoods still had dirt streets, cesspools and no sidewalks. East of Sepulveda was still considered the country and nonconforming.

With the population in the area increasing, the board of trustees became concerned about the health of the livestock farms. Through Ordinance 254, dairies were prohibited to operate without permission from the board. The following year in 1924, the board enacted Ordinance 271, which set rules and regulations for the control of foot-and-mouth disease.

The chicken farms located on Eighth and Ninth Streets, however, were still in business. Fox farms were not so lucky, for the city in 1936 acted to prohibit the farms by withholding building permits for anything that could be used for such a purpose. The city was receiving objections from residents in the area, ranging from the nauseating odors to the farms being breeding places for flies and vermin. In 1939, the city forbade mink farms to be established for the same reason. The area had been found to be a good place for the raising of fur-bearing animals in captivity for commercial markets.

Through the decades, east of Sepulveda Boulevard has experienced change and developed into residential homes, schools and churches. Gone are the farms and wide-open spaces.

Policing the Police

In 1956, the Manhattan Beach Police Department had a new chief, Jerome "Jerry" Whithers, who found himself faced with political and internal issues. In one of the first acts as chief, Jerry fired officer C.G. Hansen for misconduct, incompetence, inefficiency and failure to perform his duties as a policeman. However, after several weeks of hearings, Hansen was found not guilty of all charges. The officer resigned the department and joined the San Fernando Police Department.

Due to public insistence, Chief Withers's department began a crackdown on sexual perversion, which was taking place on the beach and in public restrooms. A two-month investigation by two undercover detectives was responsible for the arrest of thirty people on sexual charges, resulting in a 100 percent conviction rate.

Not so confident was the working atmosphere in the station. In 1957, the Manhattan Beach Civic Association asked the district attorney's office to do an internal investigation of the police department. It charged that supervisors were harassing police officers, and favoritism was being shown in the appointment of officers to higher ranks. Chief Withers held the entire force incommunicado for fifteen hours, during which time they were not allowed to call home while an investigation was conducted. With trusted supervisors, the chief conducted the investigation trying to identify those people or the person who made the allegations. The chief's findings were not made public.

By the end of 1957, the city's population was approximately thirty-two thousand, and it was clear that the overcrowded police department located in city hall needed new quarters. In order to keep pace with the steady growth, a new station was completed in 1958 at a cost of $185,000. The ten-thousand-square-foot facility was furnished with the very finest modern equipment. Law enforcement personnel occupied the new quarters in 1959, confident that the department now had the ability to keep up with increased demands.

With the move into the new quarters, the department now included three women who were hired to work the new communications desk. Due to the new hires aboard, police officers were released to work in the field. There were now thirty personnel, which included four detectives and four motor officers capable of fielding seven patrol cars at one time.

In those days, nationwide crime was on the increase. However, the Manhattan Beach Police Department had been able to keep pace with problems in town. For the first time, the city filed the department statistics with the Federal Bureau of Investigation. There were 7 robberies, 212 burglaries, 5 assaults, 106 thefts under fifty dollars, 334 thefts over fifty dollar, 87 stolen cars and no murders. The department stayed vigilant to crime while remaining active in community needs, such as filling sandbags to protect residential areas in heavy rainstorm flooding. The force was well acquainted with the town and its people, creating an easygoing relationship.

The decade of the 1960s began with the residents of the city enjoying one of the lowest crime rates in the country. However, the demand on law enforcement was about to change. Increasing criminal mobility, a larger population and complex police procedures would alter law enforcement operations to a greater degree than any other city service.

SPORTS AND CIVIC GROUPS

With the use of school buildings, playgrounds, tennis courts, the swimming pool and other school-owned facilities, the citizens enjoyed many community recreation programs. New lighting systems and baseball field improvements at Live Oak and Manhattan Heights made it possible for expansion of Little League, Pony League, softball and football. Premier Little League was the original little league in Manhattan Beach, with its field located on the old Brown Ranch, now Polliwog Park. Today that field, which was completed in 1955, is still known as Premier Field. In 1954, the league was incorporated by the State of California, chartered and franchised by Little League Baseball, Inc. In 1988, Premier League was incorporated into the Manhattan Little League.

Another baseball organization east of Sepulveda Boulevard was the Mira Costa League, now known as Mira Costa Baseball, with youngsters ages five to fourteen from Manhattan, Hermosa and Redondo Beach.

Prior to the formation of a little league west of the highway, the City of Manhattan Beach Recreation Department provided a baseball program. However, due to complaints about the expense of taxpayers' dollars, the program was canceled. In 1958, with the help of many volunteers and Monsignor Edmund O'Donnell, pastor of American Martyrs Church, Manhattan Beach Little League was in place for "downtown boys."

The first roster showed a total of 242 young boys who made up the complement of four major teams and ten minor teams. Due to the city's unwillingness to support the program and the recreation department's refusal to allow the school playgrounds to be used for Little League baseball games, the new league had to find a playing field.

It was Monsignor O'Donnell who felt that every young boy should have the opportunity to play baseball. With his help and enthusiasm, a field that was once the location of a pottery dump for the Metlox Company was created on the church's school grounds. The arrangement was much the same as today: the league was to improve the field, take care of it and let the grade school use the facility during school hours.

Eventually, another ballpark facility was developed on land owned by the church. O'Donnell Field was located on what is now known as Laurel Square at the corner of Laurel Avenue and Thirteenth Street.

The Little League programs were but one of the social activities that occurred in the 1950s. It was a time of many organizations receiving charters both for social and charitable work. Many are still very involved to this day: Rotary Club (1950), Liberty Village Women's Club (1950), American Association of University Women (1952), Coordinating Council (1953), Soroptimist Club (1953), Optimist Club (1954), Hermosa–Manhattan Business and Professional Women's Club (1954), Kiwanis Club (1956), Police Department Softball Team (1957), Loyal Order of Moose-Lodge 323 (1957),

Women of the Moose (1957), Knights of Columbus (1958), Manhattan Beach Junior Chamber of Commerce (1958), Friends of the Library (1958) and Dolphins (1959).

With all the activity the 1950s, it was still the beach that provided the most social and recreational activities. By the end of the decade, the city and private owners had sold the remaining beach acres to the state, so now the Manhattan Beach shoreline was truly a public beach.

Chapter 6
1960s

Flurry of Police Activity

The 1960s saw a flurry of activity in and around police departments across the county. In many cases, there was a lack of respect and appreciation for officers. In Manhattan Beach, the residential population enjoyed one of the lowest crime rates in the county. However, that was to change.

With increasing criminal mobility, a larger population and a new police station, training became a major recruitment qualification for all officers. No longer were the officers appointed by the Manhattan Beach City Council but rather were required to take a civil service examination, and new officers were sent to the County Sheriff's Academy for a period of sixteen weeks.

The salary for 80 of the first 160 hours of training was paid by the State of California. Manhattan Beach was the first city to qualify for the State Salary Reimbursement Plan. After the academy, the trainee continued his education for six weeks to two months with the assistance of an officer at the station. Officers were also selected for additional schooling at the FBI Academy in Washington, D.C., various universities and surrounding colleges.

In the course of an officer's training was the opportunity to participate on the pistol team, which in the early days had a pistol range located off Blanch Road. These teams were skilled and proficient, scoring high honors while traveling to various locations. In 1962 and 1963, the pistol team participated in twenty-four matches, losing only four of them.

However, it was not all about winning trophies and honors. With crime escalating, law enforcement was doing all it could to make the community aware of the dangers around them. One battle the department had to contain with was youth safety and the increasing rate of young people being picked up by officers for possession of drugs, sexual delinquency and municipal code violations. Having only one juvenile officer, the department reached out to the community. It was evident it needed help in making parents and the community aware of the growing drug-related problems.

Prior to the hiring of Officer Sandra Leigh, who was the first female officer in Manhattan Beach, women working in the department had office duties only. In 1966, Betty Andrews graduated from the police academy in Los Angeles and became the second policewoman to serve on the local force, replacing Leigh as the city's juvenile division officer. By the end of the year, the department was experiencing an average of seven hundred juvenile offenses a year, and narcotics violations were on the increase.

Safety became everybody's business, with many education programs, such as bicycle and motorcycle safety, being put into place. Another program was the incorporation with the schools, the Dolphins Club and the police department to bring a program of traffic safety into the classroom. In 1967, a professionally organized puppet show was shown to every kindergarten and first-grade child in the Manhattan Beach school system. The show depicted numerous safety scenes, and at its conclusion, a uniformed officer known as "Officer Friendly" appeared. Children in the primary grades got to know good safety habits and the police officers, instilling the idea that a police officer was someone they could go to in time of need.

At the high school level, the officers played additional roles in the Accident Prevention Program. Each year they assisted the local high school in traffic education, hoping to improve driving habits of the young students. Information from speeding to driving under the influence to reckless driving was available. Not only did the program promote safety awareness, but it also built a positive image for the police department in the community.

PIER PRESERVATION

During the late 1960s, the community became increasingly interested in the maintenance and preservation of the municipal pier and surrounding beach area. In 1957, the Manhattan Beach City Council had approved the deed

In 1962, it was not only the pier that received damage from a winter storm but also a caved-in parking lot and sand inches deep on parts of The Strand.

transfer of the pier to the State of California for the sum of one dollar, along with the ability to retain mineral and oil rights. Los Angeles County assumed maintenance of the pier with conditions: no night usage, it had to be closed during storms and no cars on the pier.

There were elements of pier work done by the state that brought attention to other surrounding beach areas. It was not only the years that took a toll on the municipal pier and The Strand but also the weather. Powerful wave action was so strong that sand was driven across the bike path, to the entry of the pier and up onto The Strand.

In 1968, City Manager Gayle T. Martin did a detailed analysis of the initial construction, history and financial consideration for rehabilitation of The Strand. The report revealed that initial construction of The Strand started in 1917 at a cost of less than $100,000, which was financed by special assessment districts. After serving for more than fifty years as one of the city's prize assets, it had reached a point of deterioration that was both unsightly and hazardous. At the time, the city manager had recommended that the city council appropriate funds in the coming budget year for engineering studies to determine necessary action and estimate the project cost.

Another issue that affected The Strand in 1968 was a proposal by the Underground Utilities Study Committee. It was proposed that the "beach area"—bounded by Highland Avenue on the east, The Strand on the west and the entire length of Manhattan Beach Boulevard from its most easterly point in the city to where it connected with the beach area—have its utility wires be placed underground. This area was to become the city's first underground district, known as "the T."

It would be many years and many arduous delays before the first Undergrounding Assessment District, 85-1, was approved. In 1989, the city council passed appropriate resolutions to create the area within First Street, Bayview Drive, Eighth Street and The Strand, a much smaller area than the original proposal.

Not everything was as worrisome as undergrounding. In 1966, Charlie Saikley introduced a new venue to the activities held at the pier. Charlie started the first girls' volleyball team. Practice took place at Live Oak Park, which at the time provided a sand area now used as the park's "Tot Lot." It was Charlie who saw the practical need to lower the volleyball net height in order for the young ladies to play. Prior to 1970, Manhattan Beach had the only courts set in this manner.

In 1968, the Sixth Annual International Surf Festival took place, and a year later, the Hyperion Outfall Serenaders were formed. In 1975, by city council proclamation, the group became the city's official Dixieland band.

However, with all the fun and games, the police department was still working to promote a positive image to the community by switching to all-white vehicles and doing all it could to make the community aware of drug abuse. In 1967, many saw Manhattan Beach as a quiet, low-profile community. But to others, it was labeled as the reigning party town on California's southern coast. It was at this time that George Jung became a problem for the town's police department.

George wanted wealth, and in the temper of the times, what better way than go into the drug trade? To George, this was the place—close to the airport and to the Mexican border. There is little wonder that this young man of the 1960s generation thought he had found paradise.

However, George was finally caught and sent to prison. It is said that he made approximately $100 million before losing it all. George Jung's story and his involvement with the narcotics business can be read in the book *Blow*, written by Bruce Porter, and it is also chronicled in the movie by the same name.

"Decade of Progress"

It had been said that 1955–65 was a "Decade of Progress." The International style and philosophy of design was here to stay and nowhere could it have been better portrayed than in the modern "flying wing" design by Rissman & Rissman Associates. The building was located on 1.5 acres of land at the corner of Valley Drive and Sepulveda Boulevard. Once known as the Pen & Quill Hotel, it was originally built by Robert Reuben, who owned the Pen & Quill Restaurant. The hotel was physically connected over Valley Drive to the restaurant by an enclosed walkway.

Many years later, the appearance of the building changed dramatically after Peter Post and his family purchased the hotel. The structure was transformed visually into a nineteenth-century European manor house, with its shuttered windows, small gabbled darners and tile roof. The interior had the décor of the Victorian era: cut-glass windows, mosaic floors, classical support columns and crystal panels from the original Lloyd's Brighton Bank in England, giving the ambiance of a period of gracious living. Today, the grand hotel has been returned to its original modern motif.

The community continued to grow with the Manhattan Beach City Council and staff being assisted by twenty-eight men and women on four commissions and one Board of Zoning Adjustment Commission.

Formed in 1964, the Beautification Commission, consisted of seven members, served to keep the city landscaped and upgraded. The commission also presented monthly and quarterly awards to both homeowners and businesses for their efforts in beautification to their properties. The commission was later dissolved.

The other commissions—planning (seven members appointed by the mayor), parking (three members) and parks and recreation (six members)—are still in service today. The Board of Zoning Adjustment (five members) was dissolved on July 1, 1993, its duties being taken over by the planning commission.

From 1955 to 1965, with an increased volume of building and a philosophy of pay-as-you-go, the tax rate established by the city council decreased. The decade saw many capital improvements, both public and residential: street construction, water and drainage systems, parks and playgrounds, sidewalks and a whole range of senior citizen activities. However, there were still parcels of land to be developed east of Sepulveda.

There were five Standard Oil storage oil tanks located east of Sepulveda and west of Aviation Boulevard, between Marine and Rosecrans Avenue.

In 1967, the Standard Oil Tank farm began to change when TRW, Inc. purchased a parcel of the farm. A preliminary master plan was presented to the city, and after approval, the 150,000-square-foot, two-story TRW building was built on Aviation. It was at this time the Nishi tract was developed. By mid-July 1968, thirty-one new homes were in the framing stage of construction. That same year, with the landscape saturated with houses and building permits at an all-time high, the city council directed the city manager to establish an environmental control officer.

The new officer would serve on the city manager's staff. The purpose of the job was to receive complaints and take action to assure the preservation of the community's amenities, as well as maintain clear, orderly residential and business neighborhoods. The city thus embarked upon a new and different approach to preserving the community's character.

BEACH—CITY PARKING WOES

While the police had its hands full with developing plans to educate the public as to the criminal activities in town and the expanding population of residents and summer visitors, there was an ever-growing increase in parking problems. In 1967, with a population of 36,538, there were 30,377 parking citations issued, making it almost beyond the ability of the Manhattan Beach Police Department to keep up with the acute parking problems. Tourists as well as local residents were competing for parking spaces. Part of the problem was the 400 percent annual escalation of motorcycles.

It was not only the downtown area that felt the parking congestion but also the Rosecrans/Highland Avenue area. Properties adjacent to city-owned land were purchased to form an off-street parking lot. Part of the project was an agreement with Southern California Edison Company to permit the city to use land north of Rosecrans for vehicle access and public parking.

Other parking projects took place, including the widening of Manhattan Beach Boulevard, the Valley Drive extension from Manhattan Beach Boulevard to Tenth Place adding more parking spaces for the downtown area and diagonal parking on Manhattan Avenue.

As the 1960s wound down, the physical improvements in the community were numerous and outstanding. One of the largest projects was the completion and dedication on April 13, 1967, of the $250,000 Public Services Facility at Bell Avenue. The development of the Public Services

Facility was financed by the sale of city land. Prior to the Bell Avenue location, the public service yard occupied the land between Sixth and Eighth Streets on Sepulveda Boulevard. The new facility improved service, added storage and created a better working environment.

A 210- by 10-foot-wide concrete loading dock for storage of items like water pipes and heavy pipe fittings was constructed, as well as an additional parking area, rack and cabinet storage. Previously, such equipment was stored on the ground at the four city-owned lots at the Peck Avenue Reservoir site.

The public works department was charged with the responsibility of providing and maintaining basic community facilities and services for the residents and business establishments within the city. The more obvious of these services are water distribution, refuse collection and street and park maintenance.

The fire department also experienced growth in 1967, with five new firemen added during the year. Many hours were devoted to giving these men the basics of fire protection and first aid, which were department requirements.

With all the activity within the city departments, the Manhattan Beach City Council continued to work to improve the taxpayers' concerns. Ordinance No. 1060 was adopted, which stated that a property owner could not divide a lot without going through established procedures. For some, the measure came fifty years too late, but many believed it to be better late than never.

Other actions included a Manhattan Beach Chamber of Commerce–sponsored code of ethics for businessmen; a requirement that establishments selling alcoholic beverages had to apply for a conditional use permit; a directive for the chief building inspector to eliminate all zoning violations and to take action to eliminate "bootleg" apartments; and adoption of the Land Use Element of the General Plan.

The Undergrounding Utilities Committee was reactivated, working for the removal of overhead wires and poles, and a refuse container ordinance was adopted that required all new structures to provide an enclosure for refuse containers. With such ordinances and findings, the city council worked to stem the tide of urban blight and to control density.

The Christmas Tree

Through the years, city departments have been involved in various community holiday events. In December 1969, the police department assisted second graders from the city school district in decorating a special

Christmas tree. Working to promote a positive image for the department, the author had asked a reluctant city manager to purchase a living pine tree, which was to be planted in Polliwog Pond Park.

The assignment to help find the tree was given to Captain Hugh O'Brien of the Manhattan Beach Police Department. After much searching, the first thirteen-foot evergreen tree was planted by the Public Works Department on the knoll just north of Manhattan Beach Boulevard in what is now know as Polliwog Park.

Ornaments were made by the students at school and then taken to the park on a given afternoon. During the tree trimming ceremony, older children under the sponsorship and direction of the Youth Council sang carols. Police Chief Crumly also accepted the idea of having the department bring Santa Claus to the program in a black-and-white patrol car and to have officers participate as helpers.

The mayor, members of the chamber of commerce and Santa Claus were honored guests. The chamber supplied the balloons, with Jo's Candy Cottage supplying a candy cane to each youngster. For many years, various school classes participated in the annual Christmas tree ceremony.

The event no longer takes place, but the tree still stands on the Polliwog Park knoll, along with several other evergreens.

Chapter 7
1970s

New City Hall

With the demolition of the old city hall at a cost of $5,600, the idea of a new facility had been in the making long before the 1971 earthquake. In 1956, it was felt that a new city hall was needed. However, not until the damage from the quake did the plan go into effect.

The Manhattan Beach City Council recommended to the Manhattan Beach–Los Angeles County Civic Center Authority that the low bid of $1.7 million from Willens & Bertisch Company be accepted for the construction of a new, 27,474-square-foot building. The new structure was built at the same location where the old city hall, which was completed in 1916, stood for fifty-five years at Fifteenth Street and Highland Avenue. This new structure became the fourth city hall in town since the city's incorporation in 1912.

The first city hall occupied the Meacham's building, one of the first structures on Manhattan Beach Boulevard between Manhattan Avenue and Ocean Drive. Number two was housed on the top floor of the Sadler Building located on the southeast side of Marine Avenue and The Strand.

The notable design was an extreme departure from the architecture of the previous structure, and many residents wished to see the old building saved. However, it was time to move on. The upper level of the new structure offered an inviting air of open space and housed the business offices, while the innovative City Council Chambers were located on the lower level. Another amenity located on the lower level was a 4,800-square-foot emergency operating center with the capacity of supporting fifty people for up to two weeks in the event of a catastrophic disaster.

On the wall of the foyer staircase leading to the lower level was a mural presented to Manhattan Beach for the new city hall by the City of Culiacan, Sinaloa, Mexico. The work symbolized "the union of men for the creation of the Greek god Prometheus." The work was created by world-renowned Mexican artist Miguel Angel Velazquez. The mural is still there. However, many years ago the artwork was covered by a curtain due to a difference in interpretation.

Heidtsmidt/Mounce/Associates, the same architectural firm that designed the new city hall, also designed the new county library, located at 1320 Highland Avenue. This addition to the civic center replaced the old library, which was located on the corner of Valley Drive and Fifteenth Street, now the location of the downtown post office and chamber of commerce.

The library, with 12,150 square feet, had much the same exterior design as the new city hall and provided a spacious interior, more light and an airy atmosphere for its patrons. Both new structures were dedicated to the city on November 1, 1975.

While the new city hall construction was taking place, another facility had already been completed. For years, the downtown merchants and shoppers had been demanding more parking facilities. In 1971, located at Morningside and Twelfth Street, the N.R. ("Bob") Kuhn Memorial structure was put into service and provided 147 more parking spaces in the downtown area.

Other capital improvements, such as the widening and installation of landscaping in the center strip of Rosecrans Avenue; beautification of Sepulveda Boulevard; the completion of the Manhattan Heights Community Building; and a portion of the median strip of Artesia Boulevard from Aviation to Sepulveda were all accomplished on a "pay-as-you-go" basis.

Elements were also being added to improve the communication system between city government and residents. In 1972, the city council approved and released the first city newsletter. However, the city manager's newsletter had been published for the previous sixteen years and revealed a very transparent view of the city's activities, being published twice a month and sent to those who had subscribed.

The new newsletter was sent to twelve thousand homes at no cost and represented a significant change in format. The first issue was a detailed recap of the plans for the new city hall and, much like today, dealt with issues such as budget, free recreation programs, dog problems, environmental control, planners pondering parking/density issues and The Strand rehabilitation.

General Plan Initiated

By the 1970s, the city consisted of 1,957 acres, excluding 475 acres of right-of-way. About 61 percent of the land was designated single-family residential, and preserving the single-family character of the community has always remained a goal. As late as 1948, the summer population was double that of winter months.

Zoning was first introduced into the city in 1923. In 1941, the first comprehensive zoning ordinance was adopted, identifying ten zoned districts. Until 1953, when Ordinance No. 675 was adopted, the land east of Sepulveda Boulevard was zoned for agricultural use. By 1957, a five-member Board of Zoning Adjustment was established for the purpose of having applications for variances, lot splits, various conditional and special use permits.

In 1965, a major reorganization of the city structure created an administration assistant position in the city manager's office. Mr. R. Kenneth Fleagle, who was also the secretary to the planning commission, had the responsibility for planning and zoning and was given the assignment to prepare a general plan for the city. The city's history indicated that the city was never planned; it just developed.

Over the years, many ordinances have been introduced, but not until the Government Code of the State of California ordered the planning commission, which had been created in 1948, to prepare the physical development of the city, did much planning take place. A Master Plan had been proposed to the planning commission in 1959, but it was not adopted due to political reality interference.

The 1970s started with a comprehensive General Plan prepared by the city planning staff, which contained twelve community goals and objectives. The plan was approved and adopted by the planning commission, as well as, the city council.

With the adoption of the General Plan, which served as a guideline for the development of the city, there were also more restrictions put on the homebuilders. For example, stiffer regulations were placed on deteriorating structures with absentee owners and irresponsible tenants. City officials, as well as residents, had great expectations for the new decade and future guidelines for the upgrading of property and new developments.

In early 1970, the city came under the California Zone Conservation Act after the voters approved Proposition 20. The act established a statewide Coastal Commission charged with the adoption and implementation of a coastal zone plan to conserve the national resources of the coastal area. The act also influenced the construction and remodeling of many homes along the coastline. In Manhattan Beach, the affected areas were located between Pacific Avenue and mean high tide, though in later years the east land boundaries were drawn closer to Valley Drive.

The earthquake of February 1971 had another grave impact on the city. The city hall, which had been built in 1916 at a cost of $12,640, was extensively damaged. Ultimately, the aging structure had to be demolished.

On August 30, a ceremony was held at the city hall site to bid farewell to the fifty-five-year-old landmark. Actor Hal Peary, who lived on Marine Avenue and was well known for his radio role as the "The Great Gildersleeve," gave the eulogy in his position of honorary mayor of Manhattan Beach. In September, at a cost of $5,600 and with many demolition difficulties, the structure was razed. In order to maintain city business, city employees were housed in temporary portable trailers located on the city's parking lot at Valley Drive.

THE STRAND

The Strand has been thought of as a historical landmark from its inception. First constructed of wooden boards, it was maintained by residents who when out for a stroll carried a small pail of nails and a hammer, used to secure loose boards. In 1914, the city fathers worried about sidewalks and lighting. This gave way to residents being assessed twenty-five dollars for major improvements. Construction of a fifteen-foot concrete walkway, which was lined with ornamental lighting, helped improve The Strand from First to Thirty-seventh Street.

During World War II, The Strand was a transport road for the U.S. Army, until trucks demolished two lampposts. The city forbade multi-axle vehicles along the walkway and billed the military fifty dollars for each of the two lampposts. However, jeeps could still drive on The Strand.

In 1963, the Manhattan Beach Council appointed the Advisory Citizens' Beautification Commission due to a growing movement to consider aesthetics in the community. In 1970, the Beautification Element was incorporated in the city's General Plan. The document contained eleven proposals for improving landscape elements in Manhattan Beach. The improvements to The Strand were to be developed by phasing the work over a period of four years.

The first Strand south of the Center Street, now Manhattan Beach Boulevard. Small buildings on The Strand housed the first real estate office while the building to the upper right became city hall.

In 1972, the city council awarded contracts for the initial phase of The Strand Rehabilitation Project. Approximately 17 percent of the concrete walk surface was removed and replaced, as was the existing lighting system. Due to the fact that many light globes had been broken, forty poles and twenty new fixtures were installed. New curbing along the westerly edge of The Strand was also completed. By 1973, decorative benches and refuse containers had been delivered and installed.

While The Strand work was being done, final plans for construction of the nineteen-mile Coastal Bicycle Path along the beach were underway. The path in Manhattan Beach basically followed the old Pacific Electric Railroad (P&E) right-of-way. The area became available for a path in 1941, after the 139 miles of Oceanside rail tracks were removed. However, the new coastal bike path was not dedicated until 1976.

People in town were worried the P&E right-of-way would become a commercial blemish to The Strand. The danger was averted when the council ruled that the land, which had been valued at $180,000 in the city limits, could only be used for beach activities and bathing.

In 1972, one of the most exciting events that the council endorsed was the Old Home Town Fair, which first took place October 20 and 21, 1973, at Live Oak Park. A committee made up of several ladies intended to capture the spirit of the community and have "old time fun at old time prices."

A section of The Strand in the 1960s prior to the 1972 Strand Rehabilitation Project.

Among the many activities were three-legged races, pie-eating contests, a dunking tank, a saltwater taffy pull, a kissing booth and marble games. There was a picnic, ice cream social, a Saturday night street dance on Valley Drive and, naturally, sarsaparilla. Applications for booths began at five dollars for a roving vendor and went up to twenty dollars for a ten-by-ten space, and applications were available at the recreation department. Artists' work had to be their own, and applicants had to live in Manhattan Beach.

The success of the first fair, which attracted an estimated ten thousand visitors, was hailed as the year's highlight. This success brought about an increase of the committee members, which rose to eleven the second year. Now known as the Hometown Fair, the event continues today at the same location during the first weekend of October.

WOMEN IN POLITICS

In the annals of American history, prior to the ratification of the Nineteenth Amendment, women's place in politics had been greatly limited.

In 1909, women in Manhattan Beach could not vote. However, they did have a great deal to do with the incorporation of the town. By 1911, the women of California had received the right to vote and all of the women who had worked so hard for the city's incorporation cast their ballots.

After ratification of the Nineteenth Amendment, women engaged in new careers. More women went to college and became leaders in their professions. However, the number of women partaking in federal or local politics was still negligible. During the 1930s in Manhattan Beach, women were deeply involved with social welfare activities. There was little thought of political office.

Women knew they had contributed to the war effort and they had the potential to influence the domestic scene. More women than ever found themselves engaged in political rolls. Suffragists contended that women were equal to men and should enjoy the same political rights.

On April 8, 1952, Mrs. Ruth M. Gorman became the first woman elected to the Manhattan City Council. However, she never became the city's mayor.

By the 1970s, time had come for the community to realize the importance of having a female viewpoint on the Manhattan Beach City Council, as women's influence on legislation became more evident. Since the incorporation of Manhattan Beach in 1912 with the first elected board of trustees, there had been, prior to 1972, seventy-one men and only one woman on the city council.

On April 9, 1972, the second elected woman, Mrs. Joan Dontanville, was seated on the city council. Mrs. Dontanville, in 1975–76, became the first woman to serve in the nine-month rotating position of mayor.

Joan Dontanville's election opened the door of opportunity for those women who followed in her footsteps. To date, there have been eight female Manhattan Beach mayors, including the author, Connie Sieber, Pat Collins, Joan Jones, Linda Wilson, Joyce Fahey and Portia Cohen.

For women with a passion for public service, the city clerk's office was an excellent choice. In Manhattan Beach, six women have served in that position. In 1976, Mrs. Jean McMillan was elected city clerk and was a powerful influence through her community service.

THE LIGHTER SIDE

On the lighter side, away from the politics and community service, were the activities for relaxation. Much like today, residents enjoyed a walk along The Strand or swimming in the surf. In 1914, Mrs. Corinne Wells, while diving and swimming from a skiff anchored offshore, experienced a memorable adventure. She was wearing a rainbow-tinted, silk "tango" bathing suit that shimmered as she glided through the surf. The flashing of the silk suit delighted two mischievous pup porpoises. They flipped over the gunwale of the skiff and gave chase. In a moment, they were playing about the frightened swimmer, arcing ahead of her as their ancestors did to guide the way for the mermaid figureheads of the ancient figure ships.

Mrs. Wells was an excellent swimmer, verified by the lifeguard, and made short time in covering the fifty feet to the shoreline. With the assistance of Mr. C.D. Armstrong, who waded into the surf to drive the porpoises off, Mrs. Well was once again on dry land and free from her playful friends.

Over the years, young women in Manhattan Beach have pursued many competitions at the beach, including beauty contests, aquaplane races, paddleboard races and volleyball tournaments, to name a few. During the '40s, it was accomplished competitive swimming. One such young woman was Cathy Davis, known as Joan Bendix, who was a competitive swimmer in her early career and later worked as a swimming instructor with Esther Williams. In 1948, she won two California championships in the one-hundred-meter backstroke, as well as being one of the first to test Jacques Yves Cousteau's new aqualung device, which was quite an experience. The device had been tested in the Mediterranean, but not in the United States. Cathy was asked to go to Catalina with several other divers to test the device. Here they saw the splendor and beauty at twenty-five feet below the surface of the water. She and her diving partner also tested the aqualung at night using flashlights to explore the deep. It was overwhelming being where few people could go. Through these tests, scuba diving became a reality for people both young and old around the world.

Cathy went on to have many other adventures relating to swimming, as did several other residents from this community, including Mrs. Frank Valenzuela, mother of five, who competed in paddleboard races, and other women who challenged the rough waters of the Catalina Channel.

Over the years, there have been many young women from Manhattan Beach who have proven themselves in the field of various aquatic and beach sports to become recipients of Olympic gold medals.

Chief Charles W. Crumly

There were many changes and additions occurring in the early 1970s. With a population in the city of approximately thirty-five thousand, the Manhattan Beach Police Department consisted of fifty-three policemen, each with a starting salary of $930 a month. These figures had changed considerably since 1951, when the population was twenty thousand and sixteen policemen received a monthly salary of $275. An officer still had to buy his uniform and weapon, but by 1975, the department provided each officer with safety equipment and a Smith & Wesson Model 67 stainless steel revolver.

By 1969, the department was under the leadership of Chief Charles W. Crumly, who reorganized the station and brought it into the age of the computer. In October 1971, the Technical Services Division began training for online operation, scheduled for January 1972. The chief also reorganized the Police Officer Reserve program, which required all new candidates to be between twenty-six and forty-five years of age, weigh a minimum of 145 pounds and be a resident of the city.

The department was changing in other ways, with several of the longtime members of the team leaving. One of them, Officer Bob Carstens, joined the department in 1948. Before the station had a place for reloading gun shells, Carstens did the job in his garage. He was referred to as a "cop's cop" and "an all-around great officer." Another officer, Assistant Chief Justus A. Smith, who joined the department in 1946, retired in 1974.

Following the retirement of Chief Crumly in 1974, Captain Hugh H. O'Brien was appointed Manhattan Beach's eighth police chief. He had been on the force since 1954, after serving with the El Segundo Police Department for two years. He rose through the ranks quickly with a wealth of street smarts and education.

Like his predecessor, O'Brien was interested in community relations. He started a speaker's bureau, which provided officers the opportunity to speak at PTAs and service clubs. He also created the ride-along program for the community, enabling them to become better acquainted with the officers and their law enforcement operations. It was felt by many of the officers that O'Brien had a true feeling for the personnel who worked for him. Chief Hugh O'Brien retired from the department in 1980. (More information about the police department can be found in *Images of America: Manhattan Beach Police Department* by Jan Dennis.)

Another service put into place in this time frame was the paramedic program by the Manhattan Beach Fire Department. The city had been providing emergency ambulance service since 1942, being the fifth municipality in the South Bay to do so. In 1973, six firemen started their five-month training program. The aim of the paramedic project was to provide quality mobile intensive care service to the community by upgrading the knowledge and skills of existing emergency services in the area.

In August that year, the city put its first paramedic unit into operation. The $13,000 van was obtained through contributions from community residents and city funds ($11,000). The sophisticated equipment was used by the fire department paramedic teams.

To help Manhattan Beach's sister city, the fire department donated a surplus fire engine to augment the badly under-equipped fire department in Culiacan, Sinaloa, Mexico. The Sister City Program began in 1963, when the Manhattan Beach City Council appointed a Sister City Committee. By 1971, bylaws were adopted and a full slate of officers was elected. Friendships between adults and young students from both cities have developed, with many exchanges of ideas and cultural events. Over the years, the city remained involved in the Sister City Program.

POWER, PARKS AND HEROES

As the mid-1970s moved forward, so did the concern from power companies that were urging voluntary cutbacks of electricity and national gas usage. Some governmental agencies were pushing laws limiting energy usage and regulating hours of store operations. In Manhattan Beach, solving the energy crisis was thought of as a citywide endeavor. All were asked to do their share. The city produced a list of ideas on how to conserve energy: turn off holiday lights, turn down thermostats, reduce lighting wattage and eliminate unnecessary travel, to name just a few of the suggestions.

Though there may have been a gas and energy shortage, the development of homes in the community continued. In 1974, fifteen modern, two-story, single-family homes were constructed on a parcel of land located north of Second Street between Meadows and Rowell Avenues. This site, once a tree nursery, was part of the old Cardenell Ranch. Today, the area is known as Carriage Place.

In 1976, Laurel Square, located at the corner of Thirteenth Street at Laurel Avenue and Church Street, become the first Planned Units Development

(PUD). The site had been previously occupied by a Little League baseball field and owned by the American Martyrs Church. The project contained fourteen individual homes, including public areas with a swimming pool and sauna, recreational room, sidewalk and a garden gazebo.

Another scheduled construction was the development of Polliwog Park. The three-phase plan, when finished, represented an investment of about $500,000 for the largest park in the city. The approximately thirty-five-acre park, owned by the Manhattan Beach School District, was designed around a theme of "naturalness." The use of concrete was to be kept to a minimum, while walkways and retaining walls were to emphasize the natural theme. Many community organizations and clubs participated in the planting of trees and flowers and in building playground equipment.

Among other community activities, the first-annual South Bay Medal of Valor Awards Luncheon took place during that time. Also there was City Spruce-up Weekend, which encouraged homeowners and businesses to improve their environments. The community took part in the National Bicentennial, while the recreation department expanded its theater productions at Joslyn Community Center. The city received money from the Title VI Comprehensive Employment and Training Act to fund more jobs for unemployed residents, and the city council decided to consolidate various small and specialized committees into a new Public Works Commission. Finally, a city bus system was put into place as an experiment.

It was at the time that the city's General Plan Land Use Classification for Standard Oil Company's tank farm was being discussed. The approximate 190 acres at one time contained five oil storage tanks, the largest of which was the size of the Los Angeles Coliseum. One of the tanks located near Aviation Boulevard became the site for a TRW building.

With the abandonment of the tanks by Standard Oil, the area was considered for alternate use such as residential, commercial and light industrial. The property represented 12 percent of the community land mass. In 1979, the city made the announcement that a development company became owners of the Standard Oil Tank Farm. The first phase of redevelopment began by filling in the underground storage tanks and grading forty acres for a shopping center.

As the 1970s came to an end, building construction in Manhattan Beach continued apace in spite of reported slowdowns in other parts of the nation. Approximately forty-six new homes were built in the city, and a tremendous amount of remodeling to existing dwellings occurred. The architecture featured many of the styles and design of previous years. Old was new again. The estate industry indicated approximately 1,215 homes were sold in Manhattan Beach throughout the decade.

Chapter 8

1980s and After

Manhattan Village

One of the most controversial plans throughout the 1980s was the development of the Manhattan Village site. In the early years, Standard Oil had the idea of developing the world's largest refinery on the site. However, over the years, from the first ad hoc committee to the community and its residents, everyone had different ideas for the property and the abandoned oil storage tanks. Concepts included a graveyard, a regional wilderness park and a lake that could accommodate paddle boating and sailboating.

In 1979, the groundbreaking commenced on a four-year project, the last major residential and commercial development in Manhattan Beach. The concept included a shopping center, residential area, business park, open space, a golf course and other amenities.

By the spring of 1982, 40 of the original 187 acres had been transformed into a 450,000-square foot, master-planned commercial center called the Manhattan Village Shopping Center. The Haagan Land and Development Company had the classic Spanish style of architecture incorporated throughout the entire project: mission tile roofs, heavy plastered walls, rough-hewn wood and old, used timbers from California landmarks such as Fisherman's Wharf in San Francisco. These elements provided a warmth and personality of design. Its 1,860-space parking lot incorporated 566 mature trees and shrubs.

The shopping center included several individual retail stores, banks and restaurants, as well as an enclosed mall. The mall had been Phase II of the development with an industrial and modern design. Phase III included the business park, recreational facilities and the residential area.

The building of the residential acreage provoked several questions, such as whether the area be gated and how to solve the methane gas problem. Methane was found under the residential area, causing a moratorium of home sales and a lawsuit brought in regard to affordable housing on the site. By the mid-1980s, many issues had been resolved, and over the years, more facilities were constructed on the remaining site. A hotel, golf course, country club and senior housing all became a reality.

With an expansion of private residences and additional businesses being constructed in the community, a concern about safety developed. In 1980, it was felt that better relations between the police and the citizens were needed. A group of six residents took on the challenge, and the Neighborhood Watch committee was formed. The hope of the committee was to have all residents participate in meetings developing a dialogue between the Manhattan Beach Police Department and homeowners, learning more about safety practices. Literature became available, and block captains were established throughout the community to inform residents how best not to become victims of crime.

As more volunteers became members of the Neighborhood Watch program, two active members were the driving force behind the Victim's Assistance Team (VAT). The purpose of the program was to listen and help victims of crime, arranging for temporary home facilities when necessary, assist victims with court appearances and give comfort wherever possible.

In 1984, the VAT program was brought to the attention of the police department. Scheduled speaking engagements were presented to local groups to explain the program and to train new volunteers. The VAT teams are on call twenty-four hours a day and work very closely with the police department.

Downtown Streetscape and Other Projects

As the 1980s moved on, the community saw Manhattan Beach City Council meetings broadcasted live on cable television. The programming began in the spring of 1984. The access channel, located in Hermosa Beach, continued to make upgrades to the equipment to improve the quality of the taped picture and sound. Residents who could not attend the live meetings at city hall could now follow the development of city government while sitting at home.

One of the significant elements the city council has to determine and approve is the yearly budget. Due to the growth of the retail market and the development of the Manhattan Village Mall, sales tax generated increased. It rose from about $1.24 million in 1979 to roughly $3.3 million just ten years later.

Another element that added to the city treasury was the assessed valuation of property. The average price of a home in 1988 was $374,149, over the $209,278 assessed in 1984, a 79 percent increase within a four-year period. The price of a home in 1979 was $138,385, which was a 170 percent increase in average price during the past decade. Home prices continued a steady climb upward to the present day, when sale prices are in the millions.

In order to maintain high quality of living standards, the city embarked on many capital projects, including the Downtown Streetscape Project, utility undergrounding in Assessment District 85-1, El Porto water system improvements, a water monitoring station, water main replacements, installation of 133 access ramps and sewer main replacements.

When it was determined in 1985 that the sewer system in the downtown area had to be rehabilitated, the city retained a firm to develop a streetscape plan for the downtown business district. An ad hoc committee was also established to resolve the wants and needs of the local merchants and residents. It would be during a special meeting on October 14, 1986, that the city council adopted the Downtown Streetscape design, after much discussion and exchange of ideas.

Lasting three years, the shoppers endured blocked streets, construction worker's trucks and mounds of dirt seemingly piled on every street corner. To enhance the sidewalks and crosswalks after the sewer work was completed, light blue tiles, with a row of darker tiles, were set by hand. Street intersections were redesigned, trees were planted and parallel parking was added to the west side of Manhattan Avenue. The Downtown Streetscape Project was a reality in early 1989.

While all the construction was taking place in the downtown area, another project was being developed by the Senior Housing ad hoc committee, which the council had appointed in 1987. In 1979, prior to this committee, the Senior Housing Foundation concluded that a significant number of Manhattan Beach elderly residents fell within "low-income" or below poverty levels.

The study stated that although many elderly homeowners (57.4 percent) had no mortgage payments, a large portion were unable to maintain their homes. It became quite clear that Manhattan Beach needed affordable housing for its senior citizens. The study and a proposal were presented to the Manhattan Beach School Board in 1983, requesting a long-term lease that would allow the Ladera School site to be transformed into a forty-unit senior citizen housing development. The proposal was turned down, but the idea of senior housing had finally been pursued.

Finally in 1991, senior housing became a reality with the development on the old Pen and Quill restaurant site at Valley Drive and Sepulveda Boulevard. The Ross Manhattan Terrace Apartments consisted of one-bedroom complexes, a community room, garages, an elevator and gardens. At this time, requirements for tenants included one person being sixty-two years or older. In later years, another senior project was developed east of the Village Mall and south of Rosecrans Avenue.

"YEAR OF THE PIER"

A great deal of activity took place in Manhattan Beach during the 1980s, from the revamping of the municipal pier to the redevelopment of the Santa Fe Railroad corridor, to an increase of large developments. In July 1984, with calm seas, thousands of visitors and residents crowded the pier as well as the beach area to catch a glimpse of the stately sailing vessels from around the world. It was part of the "Tall Ship Parade of Sails," celebrating the Los Angeles Olympic Arts Festival and Summer Olympic Games. A cannon shot at high noon signaled the beginning of the impressive nautical display.

Another element that attracted hundreds of visitors to the area was the Roundhouse, located at the end of the pier. In 1979, the Oceanographic Teaching Station, Inc. had been established and then incorporated the following year as a non-profit organization. The OTS operates the main lab and aquarium, which occupies a portion of the familiar structure. The purpose of the organization was to foster and promote an interest in the oceans, tidelands and beaches of Southern California. Thousands of visitors and students from around the area have studied marine life there, as well as the impact of human populations on the environment.

In 1984, it became apparent the pier needed refurbishing after 150 pounds of concrete had fallen on a jogger, paralyzing him. Due to the accident, the

Illustrating some of the piling of the Municipal Pier with the marine growth and vertical cracking above the waterline.

City of Manhattan Beach, Los Angeles County and the State of California were sued. After a two-year lawsuit, the county approved a record personal injury settlement of $32.26 million to the victim.

Signs reading, "Keep Out—Danger of Falling Concrete" were prominently posted. In order to catch falling debris, a chain-link fence was installed covering a good portion of the underside of the pier. The County Engineering Dive Team performed an in-depth underwater inspection of the pilings, due to reports that the pier was plagued by cracked and falling concrete with rusting, exposed girders.

Most of the pilings exhibited marine growth, vertical cracking above the waterline and telltale rust stains adjacent to the cracks. Thus, the year 1985 became known as the "Year of the Pier." There was a genuine fear for the future of the pier since the engineers' report stated it may be more cost-effective to tear down the structure and build a new one. To bring attention to the plight of the situation, a campaign called "Pier Pressure" was formed to express the conviction that the Manhattan Beach Pier was an irreplaceable landmark and a historic symbol of the city.

Discussions went on for several years. However in 1986, by a three-to-two vote, the Manhattan Beach City Council's recommendation to the California

Department of Parks and Recreation was to restore the pier rather than to construct a new one.

A few blocks to the east of the beach, between Ardmore Avenue and Valley Drive, laid the Atchison, Topeka and Santa Fe Railway Company right-of-way. Since 1888, freight cars had been rumbling through Manhattan Beach from Inglewood to the Redondo Beach Pier. When the company announced its intention of abandoning its tracks through the city, the community wondered what would become of the open space. Would the land be rezoned, redeveloped, become the location of a trolley or be left as open space?

INVESTING IN PARKLANDS

Both the Sand Dunes Park renovation and the Santa Fe Railroad right-of-way agreement took many years of negotiations. The Santa Fe trains traveled through Manhattan Beach for nearly one hundred years until the line was abandoned. In 1966, the city had received a quitclaim deed from the Atchison, Topeka and Santa Fe Railway Company for five parcels of land for the purpose of improving portions of the one-hundred-foot-wide right-of-way. The 1.7 acres were in the form of five parcels of various size and configuration: Ardmore Avenue was extended between Pacific and Palm Avenue; Valley Drive and Fifteenth Street; Valley Drive between Fifteenth Street and Manhattan Beach Boulevard; Valley Drive continued between Manhattan Beach Boulevard; Ninth Street and Valley Drive between Third and Fourth Streets.

This work however, did not disturb the rail corridor. The property known as the Santa Fe Railway right-of-way, being approximately 23.3 acres, was located between Rosecrans Avenue on the north and Duncan Street on the south and ran between Valley Drive and Ardmore Avenue.

To obtain the right-of-way, the city was to pay $4.2 million in cash and the equivalent of $800,000 in the form of four residential lots. Within the agreement, the railroad had the right to develop the remaining 2.1 acres of the right-of-way located east of Sepulveda Boulevard to Rosecrans Avenue.

On March 4, 1986, the Manhattan Beach City Council adopted the resolution that designated the 21.2 acres of right-of-way from the Sepulveda Boulevard bridge to the southerly boundary of the community as open space for recreation. By September 1986, the Santa Fe Railroad Company

In 1986, Manhattan Beach saw the end of an era with the dismantling of the Atchison, Topeka and Santa Fe Railroad Company tracks, which were laid in 1888.

had sold the tracks to an independent contractor and the dismantling began. After the salvaging work had been completed, the city's parkland increased by 40 percent, making the greenbelt the largest undeveloped open space in the community.

Shortly after the city and Santa Fe entered into a park acquisition agreement, a group of heirs of the original landowners sued the city for ownership of the greenbelt, stating that Santa Fe could not sell the acreage because the railroad did not own the property. It would take six years in the court system before the California Supreme Court ruled in favor of the city. It was now time for an improvement plan, which had been formulated several years earlier, to be put into place.

The city had been granted $1.47 million from the County Parks Board to upgrade the greenbelt. Before work was to be done, the city council wanted input from the community on improvement ideas and hired a consulting firm for $8,500 to hold public forums, which produced a variety of comments and recommendations.

There have been several amenities added to the jogging path over the years, but there was something cool about hearing the train whistle when it crossed Manhattan Beach Boulevard on its way to Redondo Beach.

THE SEVENTY-FIFTH ANNIVERSARY

In 1987, the City of Manhattan Beach Parks and Recreation Department continued to register more and more residents for classes and activities, from children's birthday parties to adult events. One of the entertaining programs was the Pier Players Theater, a group made up of many local talented actors and actresses. Sponsored by Parks and Recreation, the performances became a reality in 1975. Productions first appeared at the Joslyn Community Center, later to move into the city council chambers. Local talent graced the stage while the Pier Players won many prestigious industry awards, such as the Drama-Logue for best ensemble plays.

Another local presentation was the "Festival in the Park," celebrating its seventh showing of local artists. All artists were encouraged to enter and join a day devoted to local artists and art lovers. The event also provided live entertainment and other cultural events. However, it was the interaction with the Seventy-fifth Anniversary Committee where the Parks and Recreation staff truly reached out to the community.

The Manhattan Beach City Council in mid-1985 appointed a committee to work with staff for the planning and coordinating of the upcoming celebration of the city's seventy-fifth year of incorporation. At the same time, the council appropriated $50,000 for the development of various events, one of which was the largest parade the city had ever organized.

For many years, people believed that the incorporation date was December 12, 1912. However, that was not the case. While researching, the author found an envelope in the city hall archives containing papers on which the date 12/2/12 was written. For some unknown reason, the papers were not read and the slash was mistaken as the numeral "one." Perhaps this explains the misunderstanding. Another reason the wrong date continued to be used was that the "California Roster" in the Office of the Secretary of State in Sacramento lists the city's incorporation as December 12, 1912. The roster is not an official publication, as it receives its information from the given city. In the case of Manhattan Beach, apparently someone gave the wrong information.

A date was set for an election to be held within the proposed boundaries on November 25, 1912, to determine whether the town should be incorporated. A total of 127 votes were cast. Returns were counted on December 2, with 95 for incorporation and 32 against. At the same meeting of the County Board of Supervisors, on a motion by Supervisor Nellis, seconded with a unanimous aye, it was ordered that all the territory situated in the County of Los Angeles, State of California and within the boundaries so described was a duly incorporated municipal corporation of the sixth class, under the name and style of "City of Manhattan Beach."

On December 6, 1912, the county clerk certified that the copy of the original minutes of the Board of Supervisors, from December 2, 1912, were full, true and correct. The endorsed findings were filed in the office of the secretary of state on December 7, 1912.

An act of the California legislature entitled "An act to provide for the organization, incorporation, and government of municipal corporations," approved March 13, 1883, gave the voters the right to petition to become a city. Thanks to the frontier spirit of a few Manhattan Beach voters, the small community of beach cottages became independent of the City of Los Angeles. The self-governing body formed its own school system, police and fire departments and was determined to succeed as an independent city.

CONTROLLING GROWTH

As the 1980s came to an end, the number of housing starts continued to increase. With Manhattan Beach's new General Plan, which was adopted on 1988, 188 new units and 166 demolitions took place during an eleven-month period: 120 single-family homes, 32 duplex units and 36 multi-family units. The demolition of older single-family homes and one grade school meant that much of the city's historical architecture was destroyed. Not only were more units being constructed, but the units also contained more living square footage with a more massive, bulky profile.

The spring of 1988 brought about the imitative Proposition E, which attempted to control growth through the General Plan. An aggressive battle took place, with the opponents stating that the zoning ordinance was the place to control bulk, intensity, density, traffic, etc. In July 1989, official public hearings commenced on the Zoning Ordinance Revision Program (ZORP).

In July 1990, a group of residents called for a public action and recall of Manhattan Beach City Council and ZORP proceedings. However, it was not successful. After numerous meetings and unlimited reviews, the second reading for ZORP occurred in December 1990. Many residents expressed disappointment that the council did not do more to protect the community from overdevelopment.

It was not only a period when living units were demolished and replaced but also a time when an icon was reborn. For years, the pier had taken a beating from the weather, tides and pounding surf. In 1989, plans for the rehabilitation of the historical Roundhouse and pier began. It took years of planning and tireless hours for many residents, city and county personnel to come to an agreement on the design for the rehabilitation of the pier.

The object of the restoration for the pier, the Roundhouse and light standards was to retain the original style of the landmarks. On January 15, 1991, the council awarded a $2.39 million contract to the Kiewit Pacific Company for the first phase of the project. The second phase of work, which consisted of the Roundhouse and comfort station rehabilitation, was performed by Kevin Krauss Construction. The third phase was the replacement of the lifeguard station, which would remain the same size. However, the building would be moved to the north side of the platform at the head of the pier.

On a bright, sunny morning at eight o'clock on March 1, 1991, work began with a municipal pier groundbreaking ceremony, signaling the

In order for a crane to be driven up onto the pilings, a wooden mat was laid down creating a stable platform for the removal of the old concrete deck. The crane remained on the pier until new concrete was poured.

commencement of the project. The first structures to go were the Roundhouse, bait shack and the lifeguard tower. Not since 1922 had anyone seen the end of the pier without the familiar buildings. By February, the contractor had set up a construction yard on the sand north of the pier.

The load capacity of the pier deck would not allow the contractor to use heavy equipment, thus requiring the use of a smaller bulldozer for the demolition and removal of the debris. Exploratory holes were drilled into the deck to determine the exact location of the beams and girders in order to avoid accidentally cutting into the beams. By the end of March, the crew of Kiewit Pacific began the cutting and removal of the historic deck.

Concrete work began at the end of April 1991 and was completed in October of the same year. The concrete was loaded into a large concrete pump, which propelled the mixture over the surface of the pier. A fifty-foot safety zone was marked on both sides of the pier, prohibiting any water activity.

In May 1992, phase two of the project was awarded to Kevin Kraus Construction. This phase included rebuilding the Roundhouse and renovating the comfort station restrooms located north of the pier entry.

During the rebuilding process, crews moved the marine lab to a site on the beach in El Segundo. After a year of renovation, the pier reopened in early March. However, the Roundhouse did not open to the public until July 1992.

THE PARK SYSTEM

By February 1986, the Park Acquisition Agreement between the City of Manhattan Beach and the Atchison, Topeka and Santa Fe Railroad Company had been executed. The twenty-one acres were to become a city park, with the long-awaited 1.7-mile recreational jogging trail becoming a reality. Several years later in 1993, one of the most interesting additions placed on the parkway was the Mariposa Pathway. The permanent installation featured seven butterfly sculptures integrated within the newly improved landscape of trees, flowers and enhanced terrain.

While the parkway between Valley Drive and Ardmore Avenue was being developed, other city parks were being discussed and formulated. Approximately three acres of land located near Manhattan Village and owned by the Chevron Land and Development Company provided for the first full-sized soccer field in town. However, in later years, the field was relocated to its present location on Marine Avenue.

Over the years, there have been many phases in the development of the city park recreational system, one being the restoration of Polliwog Park Pond. Several residents wished to see the park return to an acceptable level of habitation for the wildlife that inhabited the area. After numerous discussions and the appropriation of $234,000 by the city, a capital improvement project began.

To enhance the area, a substantial number of projects had to be completed, including engineering studies, removing the existing sludge and debris from the pond, constructing a stabilizing wall around the pond basin, installing a solid cement liner and installing a water aeration and circulation system. All this increased the cost to approximately $427,000. The refurbished pond and its surroundings took roughly seven months to complete.

However, even with all the improvements, there was a sad side to the story. The question arose on what to do with the ducks and geese that nest or frequent the pond? There had been some problems in the past of wildlife being victims of violence, with nests destroyed or birds being shot.

This 1989 view looks over the refurbishing work of Polliwog Park Pond and its bird sanctuary.

Concerned residents made the city aware of the misdeeds, resulting in a fence being installed to block entrance into the affected area. But with the draining of the pond, another calamity began occurring. Many of the birds were dying. It became apparent that the remaining several dozen birds had to be moved in order for construction to continue.

City officials decided to give the public the opportunity to "adopt-a-duck," with the remaining birds transported to another park. Unfortunately, the program was not successful, due to lack of adequate promotion. The city was compelled to call the Los Angeles County Animal Control, which rounded up the creatures and had the fowl destroyed. This action caused an outcry from many of the residents. After many meetings concerning the environment at the pond, it was determined by the city council that Polliwog Park would become a wildlife sanctuary. In April 1990, a ribbon-cutting ceremony celebrated the completion of the refurbished Polliwog Park Pond project.

HISTORY OF THE PIER

A bit of history on the birth of the pier: construction of the concrete pier at the foot of Manhattan Beach Boulevard began in 1917 and was completed in 1920. The pier is reportedly the oldest existing structure of its kind on the West Coast of the United States. To celebrate the grand opening on July 5, 1920, a dance, parade and other activities were held. However, the first gathering to take place on the new pier was a memorial service held on the unfinished pier in 1918 to honor the memory of the boys who died during World War I.

The debate over a planned extension heated up in 1926 when the Manhattan Beach City Council granted a franchise to erect an addition to the pier. In 1928, Captain Larsen, who purchased the franchise, proposed a two-hundred-foot extension featuring ornamental lights, electricity, gas and water for the purpose of mooring a deep sea fishing barge as well as private yachts. In April, wooden pilings to support the extension were driven into the ocean floor.

In spite of previous repair efforts, the condition of the concrete pier has continued to deteriorate. By 1933, the piles reportedly exhibited exposed reinforcement, indicating restoration of the pier was obvious. Some work was done in 1935. With pilings washed out during the storm of 1937, the City of Manhattan Beach needed funds for storm damage repairs.

In order to obtain county funds, the city council in 1938 designated the Manhattan Beach Municipal Pier as a continuation of Manhattan Beach Boulevard (then called Center Street). It was pointed out if a pier was located as an extension of a dedicated city street, then it could logically be declared a city street. As such, it would be eligible to receive gasoline tax and road funds for repair work to replace the pilings.

Not many years later, the city would see greater damage to the pier area. In the early hours of January 9, 1940, residents in town awoke to a violent storm with high waves and winds that were extremely strong. Shortly after 4:00 a.m., the pier extension took a fatal beating when heavy surf finally wiped out nearly half of the structure. City street crews tried to free the large timbers that had broken loose, but the seas were too strong. Approximately forty feet of the extension remained. However, in February 1941, that too was swept away by another storm. The remains were uprooted, turned over on their sides and carried by heavy winds and strong current to shore almost intact.

Volleyball

One of the lighter sides of Manhattan Beach history was and still is the volleyball season. Volleyball was invented in 1895 by Mr. William G. Morgan, the physical director of the Holyoke, Massachusetts YMCA. The original name of the new game was "mintonette," derived from the word "badminton." Since the object of the game was to volley back and forth across the net, Morgan changed the name of his new game to "Volley Ball," two words. In 1950, the United States Volleyball Association changed the spelling from "Volley Ball" to volleyball, one word.

Women have been playing volleyball since the early 1900s. However, there are very few written records revealing the participation of women in the early years of beach volleyball tournament play. By 1957, there were a total of seven women's teams that took part in the Manhattan Beach International Six-Man Volleyball Tournament. The 1957 tournament drew a notable number of women to the sport.

The following year saw the first Women's Open Volleyball Tournament, which was held in Manhattan Beach on the beach north of the pier. The event drew girls from as far away as Mexico City. As interest in the game increased in the 1960s, more tournaments were organized for the ladies. There would be more attention paid to women's volleyball skills after the arrival of a new coach, Mr. Charlie Saikley.

For many, Charlie Saikley was the father of the Manhattan Beach Open. In 1966, Charlie, a young special education teacher at El Segundo High School, introduced a new venue to the activities held at the pier. Working summers with the City of Manhattan Beach since 1963, Charlie in 1965 started the first girls' volleyball team. Practice took place at Live Oak Park, which at the time provided a sand area now used as the park's "Tot Lot" for children.

The girls soon took on the challenge of competition with tournaments of their own. After moving their practice down to the pier area, Charlie saw the practical need to lower the volleyball net height. Prior to 1970, Manhattan Beach was the only court set up in this manner.

The young ladies also had a new innovation in the display of their name, the "Tyros," which was imprinted on the back of their swimwear and t-shirts, a practice that was not made popular until much later. In addition to the Tyros, Charlie coached the eleven-to-thirteen-year-old girls' team named the Pacers. Many of Charlie's protégées went on to become well-known female volleyball players, winning numerous gold medals in Olympic games, as well as being honored with other wins at women's volleyball tournaments.

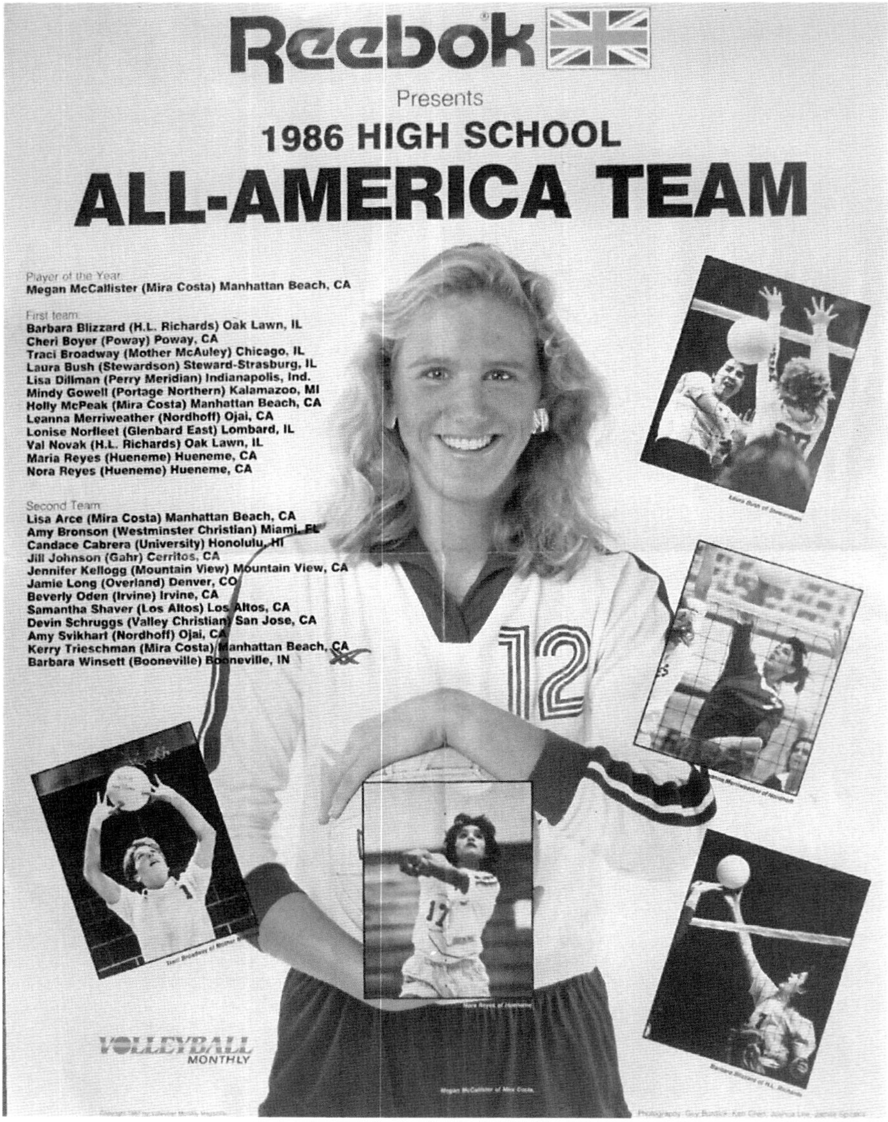

This advertisement for Reebok, which appeared in the *Volleyball Monthly*, presented the 1986 High School All-American Volleyball teams. Player of the Year was Megan McCallister, and Holly McPeak played on the first team; both girls were students at Mira Costa High School. That year, Lisa Arce and Kerry Trieschman, also from Mira Costa, played on the second team.

In 2004, to honor all the winners of the Manhattan Beach Open dating back to 1966, the city created the "Women's Walk of Fame" on the Manhattan Beach Pier. During the inauguration ceremony, Charlie Saikley was congratulated for his commitment to women's beach volleyball.

Along with the sporting talents of young women like Kerri Walsh, Misty May, Nina Matthies and Karolyn Kirby, the Manhattan Beach Pier drew one of the greatest athletes in the history of the South Bay—Kirk Kilgour. A volleyball legend, Kirk started playing the game near the Manhattan Beach Pier like many other young people.

By 1967, at the age of nineteen, he held an AA rating for men's beach volleyball, and in 1968, an AAA rating. In 1970–71, he began playing indoors on UCLA's first championship volleyball team. His volleyball uniform became the first to be retired, and his name appears in the Helms Athletic Hall of Fame. In 2002, at the age of fifty-four, Kirk Kilgour succumbed to heart failure.

Historical Preservation

From the 1900s and on to the 2000s, the growing concern by many Manhattan Beach residents was, "How big is too big?" Estate grandeur could be seen in much of the burgeoning construction throughout the community, from Spanish Mediterranean villas to Moorish-styled manors.

In sharp contrast to the previous high-tech, avant garde expressions, much of the newer architecture took on a heavy and massive appearance with little or no regard for front setback or open space. In some cases, the trend to build larger homes was being solved by combining lots, demolishing the home next door to provide more space and maximizing the square footage to gain a more dominating profile.

Over the last one hundred years, this community of just four square miles has witnessed dramatic architectural change. From the beginning, with the exception of sparse industry, the town has always been thought of as a residential community. Although its population has increased to 35,135 residents, it still remains largely residential today.

The soul of a community is its history—not only the heritage of its residents, but also that of the architecture and the land. Communities are trying to preserve their historical homes and buildings; Manhattan Beach, too, must maintain its architectural link to the past. It is through preservation that future generations will be given the opportunity to understand and

Built in 1900, this is one of the many historical homes that the Manhattan Beach Conservancy has been researching.

visualize the quality of their community. Cherishing and preserving the past also means controlling the destiny of future development.

Historical preservation is an important element in the retention of the character and soul of a community. Sadly, Manhattan Beach is losing its historical landmarks at a frightening pace. In 2006, due to the persistence and caring of a handful of residents, Ordinance 2089 was adopted to designate culturally significant landmarks. It is the goal of the Manhattan Beach Cultural Heritage Conservancy to safeguard the city's heritage by encouraging the recognition and voluntary protection of landmarks representing significant elements of local history and culture.

The Manhattan Beach Conservancy Board met with Mr. Marcello Vavala, a member of the Preservation Associates at the Los Angeles Conservancy. Marcello gave pointers as to what the group could do to help homeowners understand historic preservation better. Following is a list from the Los Angeles Conservancy and Manhattan Beach Municipal Code regarding designation of culturally significant landmarks and a rundown of the conservancy's most prevalent myths about historic preservation.

Myth #1: "If a property is designated a historical landmark, it's protected forever and can never be demolished."
Fact: Landmark designation ensures a more thorough review of demolition proposals, but it does not prohibit demolition outright. In Section 10.86.070 of City Ordinance No. 2089, the designation of a property or site as a culturally significant landmark is an honorary designation only. Such designation shall have no effect upon the property rights of the owner of the property nor curtail alteration, development or demolition of such property.

Myth #2: "Historic designation will lower my property values."
Fact: Study after study across the nation has conclusively demonstrated that historic designation and the creation of historic districts actually increase property values. Why? In part because historic designation gives a neighborhood or an individual historic site a cache that sets it apart from the ordinary property. Many buyers also seek out the unique qualities and ambiance of a historic property.

Myth #3: "If my property is designated as historic, I won't be able to change it in any way, and I don't want my property to become like a museum."
Fact: Owners of designated historic structures can make significant changes to their property. Historic preservation laws, at their essence, are not meant to prevent change, but rather to manage change. The tool to manage change is the Secretary of Interior's Standards for Rehabilitation, the nationally accepted benchmark for evaluating changes to historic structures.

Myth #4 "Preservation is an un-American violation of property rights."
Fact: Historic preservation laws no more infringe on property rights than do many other laws and rules that Americans have long accepted. Though everyone likes to believe "my home is my castle and I can do whatever I want," this statement simply doesn't reflect reality. Zoning laws prevent you from replacing your single-family home with an apartment building or a five-story vertical mansion. We should all be happy that such laws prevent our neighbors from putting a landfill or a skyscraper behind our back fence.

If you live in a condominium (or gated community,) your property rights are limited by Covenants, Conditions and Restrictions (CC&Rs), documents that can legally prevent you from owning a pet, washing a car in your driveway, or having a basketball hoop over the garage. CC&Rs are far more onerous than historic preservation laws, yet are commonly accepted even by vocal property rights advocates.

About the Author

Jan DeNike Dennis was raised and educated in the small town of Ridgefield, Connecticut. She attended Art Career School in New York City and worked for Year Publishing there. She has lived in Manhattan Beach for more than fifty years and been involved with civic activities for more than forty years.

She was elected to the Manhattan Beach City Council in 1984, after serving on the planning commission. Jan served as the second female mayor in Manhattan Beach history. Working with the city staff, she gained a great deal of knowledge about Manhattan Beach's history. This led to the publication of her first book, *A Walk Beside the Sea*, the first comprehensive history of Manhattan Beach. This book is her seventh title dedicated to her beloved city.

Dennis's dedication to the research of her community's past has resulted in a number of books that prevent the history of Manhattan beach from slipping into obscurity:

Images of America: Manhattan Beach, California. Charleston, SC: Arcadia Publishing, 2001.

Images of America: Manhattan Beach Pier. Charleston, SC: Arcadia Publishing, 2005.

Images of America: Manhattan Beach Police Department. Charleston, SC: Arcadia Publishing, 2001.

Shadows on the Dunes: An Architectural History of Manhattan Beach, California. Manhattan Beach, CA: Janstan Studio, 2001.

Skirts Across the Sand: A History of Manhattan Beach Women. Manhattan Beach, CA: Janstan Studio, 2008.

A Walk Beside the Sea: A History of Manhattan Beach, California. Manhattan Beach, CA: Janstan Studio, 1987.